To:

_____

From:

_____

Date:

_____

GRIEVING
the LOSS *of a*
LOVED ONE

A Devotional of Comfort as You Mourn

KATHE WUNNENBERG

ZONDERVAN®

ZONDERVAN

Grieving the Loss of a Loved One

Copyright © 2000, 2016 by Kathe Wunnenberg

Requests for information should be addressed to:
Zondervan, 3900 Sparks Dr., SE, Grand Rapids, MI 49546

ISBN 978-0-310-35872-5

Cover design: Kathy Mitchell

Interior design: Mallory Collins

Printed in China

16 17 18 19 20 21 TIMS 19 18 17 16 15 14 13 12 11 10 9 8 7 6 5 4 3 2

*With love and gratitude to my
husband, Rich Wunnenberg.
You inspired me through your own
grief journey to trust God.
And to you, the reader: you keep me motivated
to press on and bring purpose to my pain. May
the Father of compassion and God of all comfort
who has comforted me comfort you, and in
time work through you to comfort others.*

Contents

Contents

READING FOR
SPECIAL DAYS OR NEEDS

Special occasions, holidays, and personal circumstances may trigger your grief and expose a new dimension of living life without your loved one. When you encounter these times in your journey and desire encouragement or a fresh perspective, turn to the selected reading for that specific day or need.

Your Journey Through Grief

*L*osing someone you love through death is painful and personal. You soon learn that grief can't be confined to a method, time frame, or event; it's a process. Grief is a unique and unpredictable experience. Like the swelling waves of an ocean, grief may appear endless and crash at your soul, while at other times grief ebbs and flows. One moment you may feel engulfed by a wave of sorrow; the next moment waves of hope and acceptance lift you. Grief can be an irregular tide that frequently takes you by surprise.

How you respond to grief determines the quality and direction of your life. You can choose to allow it to drown you emotionally, or you can allow loss to enlarge you. As difficult as it is to lose a loved one, grief can deepen you as a person and increase your empathy and your trust in God. Loss can open your eyes to see the same world from a different viewpoint. In that sense, grief is a journey.

Whether you've recently suffered loss and are beginning your grief journey, you are several years into your journey, or you are somewhere in between, a void will exist in your life from losing your loved one. Each season of your life may find you blazing a new trail as you discover a different dimension of your loss. And just when you think your journey through grief has finally ended, you see a fork in the road and find yourself trudging down a familiar path that you've walked before.

Grieving the Loss of a Loved One gives you permission to be who you are and where you are in your journey. Take a moment to glance at the table of contents. You may want to use it as your compass, helping you find the section of the book that best fits your need each day or in a moment, on a special occasion, or in a season when you need encouragement. Read the book straight through, one devotion per day, or take a slower pace and meditate on one devotion for each week of the next year. You may also choose to invite others to read along with you: a friend or family member, a counselor, or a small group of fellow grievers in need of support who may use the book as a discussion guide. However you use the book, let it help you wherever you are on the journey.

If you need to cry, weep with all your heart.

If you need to vent, tell God the whole truth about how you're feeling.

If you're ready to celebrate, do it with gusto.

My hope is that you will embrace *Grieving the Loss of a Loved One* as a personal companion. Think of it as a good friend with whom you can share laughs, tears, dreams, and your innermost thoughts. Whether you read this devotional daily or as the need arises, highlight it, dog-ear it, write in it. My prayer is that it will be a tool to guide you to a deeper understanding of who God is.

I pray the stories that follow will comfort your soul and give you courage to press on in your journey. What I have written (and updated in 2015) has grown out of the personal experience of losing my infant son and three children through miscarriages, being married to a man who lost both his parents as a child, suffering through many life losses, and walking beside others who are grieving too.

I believe that God, who suffered the loss of His only Son, understands our worst pain and our darkest thoughts. Wherever you are on the journey through grief, God longs to speak to you and also to draw near to you. I hope the stories, Scriptures, prayers, and space to record your own thoughts, questions, and prayers will help bring healing and a closer relationship with the One who loves you.

I am convinced that we sometimes go through difficult experiences so we can encourage others who will later endure similar hardships. This book wouldn't have been possible without the men, women, and children who shared their personal insights and stories. I have written this book not as an expert, not as someone who has healed completely, but as a fellow griever, still on the journey. Behind the pages of *Grieving the Loss of a Loved One* is a person who can relate to at least some of what you are experiencing. And behind that person is a faithful God who is able to comfort you and in time work through you, too, to comfort others.

Part 1: Denying

YOUR JOURNEY THROUGH DENIAL

Denying: *to declare untrue, to disclaim connection with or responsibility for, to refuse to accept*

How do I manage a difficulty? Well, at first I try to walk past it. If that does not help, I try to climb over it; and when I cannot climb over it, to crawl underneath. And when that is not possible, I go straight through—God and me.
—CORRIE TEN BOOM, *CLIPPINGS FROM MY NOTEBOOK*

"Am I only a God nearby," declares the LORD, "and not a God far away? Who can hide in secret places so that I cannot see them? . . . Do not I fill heaven and earth?" declares the LORD.
—JEREMIAH 23:23–24

Journey Through the
Fog to Reality

You can't heal a wound by saying it's not there!
—Jeremiah 6:14 tlb

Shock. Disbelief. Numbness. Confusion. You may encounter some of these feelings when facing the reality of your loss. At times you may feel as if you're walking on a road through a dense fog, stumbling through the nothingness that surrounds you, searching for an escape yet finding none.

Getting fogged in was a common occurrence when we lived in Oregon. Most mornings I would peer out our family room window expecting to see fir trees and mountains, only to find they had vanished once again.

Whenever the fog rolled in, I felt out of control, thinking about airport delays and white-knuckle driving. Over time, though, I learned to cope with the eerie white vapor and to forge through it—sometimes with the help of my car's headlights. I realized the impairment was temporary, and that gave me hope to endure. By afternoon the fog would lift, and I could see clearly again.

That's how it is with grief. Our initial shock over a loved one's death may cause us to deny it or ignore it. We may feel lost, paralyzed, in limbo, somewhere between reality and a dream.

This can't be happening! you think.

But it is.

I don't want to face it!

But you have to.

Maybe not right this moment. That's okay. But if you want to journey through grief, you must look beyond the clouds created by denial and fears. With God's strength and in His timing, the fog will begin to clear, and you'll be able to see reality again. It may not be what you want to see, and it may look quite different from before, but it is a necessary part of your journey through grief.

How are you coping with your loss? When you look out the window of your circumstance today, what do you see? Are you in the fog, denying reality? Or is the fog beginning to clear to reveal a new landscape?

Lord, it's so hard to cope with what has happened. I don't want to believe my loved one is gone. I keep hoping I'll wake up and discover this is only a dream. I feel so unsure about where I am right now. I can't see what life should look like. Please help me through this part of the journey. You say that You will never leave me or forsake me and that You will be a lamp to my feet. Please guide me through this time of uncertainty and pain. Amen.

My Journey

_____

_____

_____

_____

_____

_____

_____

_____

_____

_____

_____

_____

_____

Devotion 2

GRIEF MIRAGE

*"If anyone is thirsty, let him come to me and drink. For
the Scriptures declare that rivers of living water shall flow
from the inmost being of anyone who believes in me."*

—JOHN 7:37–38 TLB

Ascene in an old Western movie depicts a cowboy
stranded in the desert without a horse. An ocean of
sand surrounds him. The sun blazes down. His mouth is
parched and dry. His canteen is empty. His only hope for
survival is to find shelter and water. He stumbles up a hill
and peers down into the valley. He can't believe his eyes.
In the distance is an oasis of water. With renewed hope, he
rushes toward it. Reaching it, he bends down to scoop up
the water in his hands. He starts to drink it—then chokes.
He spits out a mouthful of sand.

Anyone suffering from extreme thirst or mental or

physical strain can experience a phenomenon known as a mirage. It can even happen when we suffer the pain of grief.

After his wife Rachel died, I can only imagine how Jacob must have felt being left alone to parent their two sons, Joseph and Benjamin. Did he try to manage his home in the same way it was managed before, as if nothing had happened? When Jacob came home at night, did he envision Rachel running to the door to greet him, and when he opened it, no one was there? Did the familiar aroma of her perfume unleash emotions and trick his mind into believing she was still alive? How his heart must have leapt when he heard her favorite song and his mind replayed her voice singing. When he tucked Joseph and Benjamin in at night and they looked up at him with Rachel's big, brown eyes, did he see her staring back? As he lay alone in his bed at night, did he pull Rachel's pillow close and imagine her heart beating next to his? When morning rays shone on her empty side, did he see past his imagination to his new reality—life without her?

In our journey through grief, sometimes our senses can cause our minds to deceive us. A familiar sight, sound, smell, taste, or touch may trigger a memory, and for a moment we may imagine that our loved one is still here. I experienced a grief mirage while listening to voice mail messages a few weeks after my friend Debbie died. When I heard her say, "Hi, Kathe!" I nearly dropped the phone. Even though I knew it was a recorded message, in that moment, I ignored reality. I imagined my friend sitting across from me, and I listened to every word of that message and saved it. For a time, denial is a way for us to survive and cope, though we may not understand at the time that we're refusing to face our new reality. The journey through denial may affect each of us differently. Hearing or seeing imaginary things might not be your experience, but thinking that your loved one is going to call you at any moment may be.

Like the cowboy, we trudge through the heavy sand of our grief. The trek is lonely and the surroundings are desolate, but we think we're coping fine. Then we see an oasis in the distance. We run toward it and scoop up the sweet water that awaits us . . . and we nearly choke. We spit out what we thought was reality only to discover it was really a mirage triggered by our senses or memories. Our grief may cause us to have difficulty discerning reality. We may need to seek professional help or talk to another person to gain perspective.

God understands where we are. When we run to Him, He is our true oasis. When we scoop up His living water, our thirst will be satisfied with the truth.

Maybe it's time for reality to come out. Talk to another person about the pain of your loss, and run to the One who will satisfy your thirst with truth. He is waiting. Run to Him.

God, I miss my loved one. I've been wandering in the desert of denial, trying to survive the pain of my loss. I'm parched and dry. I'm thirsty for the truth. My mind and senses play tricks on me. I don't want to live in a mirage. Show me someone I can talk to who will help me cope. Forgive me for not running to You sooner. Here I am. Quench my thirst with the living water of Your Word today. Amen.

My Journey

_____

_____

_____

_____

_____

_____

_____

Devotion 3

SAILING TO THE ICEBERG OF DENIAL

"You will know the truth, and the truth will set you free."
—JOHN 8:32

On April 10, 1912, the whole world was talking about an amazing new ship, the *Titanic*, which was about to set sail from England to America. Newspapers called it "The Wonder Ship" and "The Rich Man's Special." Like a floating palace, the ship was nearly four city blocks long and as tall as an eleven-story building. Experts agreed that the *Titanic* was the safest ship ever.

Crowds lined the shore. Flags snapped in the breeze. Music filled the air. Passengers waved good-bye to their friends. The engines roared, and the ship steamed out of the harbor. The *Titanic* had begun its first voyage. No one ever dreamed that it would also be its last.

Four days later, the *Titanic* was in icy waters off the coast of Canada. Since it was late at night, most of the passengers were asleep. Suddenly the lookout saw a dark shape and sounded the alarm: "Iceberg right ahead!" But the seaman steering the ship couldn't divert the *Titanic* quickly enough, and the giant iceberg scraped along the side of the ship. There didn't appear to be much damage. Most passengers were unaware anything had even happened. Yet the terrible truth was that the massive iceberg, beneath the water's surface where no one could see, had severely damaged the ship.

During our grief journey, we may look as if we're coping with our loss. We may even start to believe that it hasn't deeply affected us and that we're unsinkable. We keep sailing through life with a smile on our face. Friends and family close to us ask us how we're really doing and whether we're denying the intensity of our feelings. Others who have experienced the loss of a loved one may even warn us to be on the lookout for the iceberg of denial. But we ignore them and sail along. The darkness closes in, and then we see it: a massive mountain of feelings, and we're heading straight for it. "Iceberg of denial right ahead!" We try to divert our life around it, but it's too late. The mound of hidden feelings beneath the surface cuts into us, and we start to sink as we face the reality of the pain of losing our loved one.

Then we learn the truth: we are not unsinkable, and we have ignored or avoided facing our loss. When we hit our iceberg of denial, we must plunge beneath the surface to examine hidden hurts. We are forced to face the damage. This is a necessary part of healing in our journey through grief: facing the truth. Unlike the *Titanic*, your iceberg will not sink you, but instead—as you take inventory of grief's damage—you can make the repairs that will allow you to stay afloat.

Facing the truth may be a process of discovery through the years. During some seasons, you will think you're coping with your loss; during others, you won't.

If you don't take an honest look at what's happening, you might crash into the iceberg of denial again. Instead, you can take safety measures to prevent that from happening often. Being truthful with yourself and others is a first step. The second step is to recognize that it's okay to feel the pain, even if it's a long time after your loss. Another safety measure is to be aware that denial does exist and that you may need a warning from God or others to help you face it. The truth may not remove your anguish, but eventually it will set you free and allow you to journey on.

God, I feel as if I'm doing okay since my loss. It hasn't affected me as I thought it would. Others are amazed at my response and how I appear to cope. Is this really the truth, or is denial hidden beneath the surface? Show me the truth today. Be my lookout and warn me as I sail through life. Prevent me from sinking. Rescue me with Your truth and help me journey on. Amen.

My Journey

_____

_____

_____

_____

_____

_____

_____

_____

_____

_____

_____

_____

_____

Devotion 4

TRUTH OR DENIAL?

Send out your light and your truth; let them
guide me. Let them lead me to your holy
mountain, to the place where you live.

—PSALM 43:3 NLT

Two women stood in front of King Solomon. One held a baby; the other clung to an empty blanket. The woman with empty arms rushed forward and told Solomon about her son's birth. She choked back tears as she shared how the other woman had given birth to a son a few days later, but her baby had died. This woman swapped the dead baby for the living baby while the new mother slept. "That's *my* baby," she moaned.

Silence pervaded the room. The king saw the pain in her eyes. He turned to face the woman holding the baby. She glared at him and shouted, "No, the living one is *my* son and the dead one is *hers*!"

What fear must have come into the heart of that baby's real mother. What boldness and denial were still in the heart of the mother whose child was dead.

Solomon commanded an attendant to bring him a sword. "Divide the living child in two, and give half to the one and half to the other."

"Oh, my lord, give her the living child and don't kill him," cried the woman with empty arms. "Divide him!" said the other.

The truth couldn't be denied. The king, who was the wisest of judges, knew by the two mothers' words who was the real mother.

I can imagine how grateful that woman was as she reached for her baby and held him once again in her arms. Her tears turned to smiles, and the heaviness in her heart was replaced with joy.

But what about the other woman? Was she really cruel-hearted and vindictive, or was she a desperate, grieving mother who would do anything to have her baby back?

What shock and pain this mother must have felt when she realized that her baby was dead. Did she convince herself he was only sleeping and would wake up soon? How tormenting for her to hear the other baby's healthy cry. No one would understand the anguish she felt. She couldn't face her loss. I wonder if she thought that just being near what she longed for would lessen her pain.

Perhaps, clutching her lifeless baby, she tiptoed into the room where everyone was sleeping. She bent down and peeked at the tiny breathing bundle. It felt so familiar. Maybe she thought, *I'll pick him up and hold him for just a few minutes*. She gently laid down her baby and scooped up the living baby into her arms. She didn't remember how long she held him or what happened next. All she knew was joy returned to her heart and a sense of relief that the death was just a terrible nightmare.

I'm not condoning this mother's actions. Yet I can relate to her pain and understand how grief can drive us to do, think, or say strange things. My brother and his wife had a healthy baby boy just a few days before my son was born and died. Although I was excited for them, the first few times I saw my nephew, he reminded me of what I longed for but didn't have. Sometimes when I held him, I would imagine that he was my son and allow myself to feel the joy of new motherhood, even if only for a few moments.

Through the years, I've watched my nephew grow into a bright, handsome, athletic young man who spoke at his high school graduation and is now entering adulthood. He continues to be a sweet reminder to me of the age or stage my son would be and is a comfort to my grieving soul.

Fantasizing that your loved one is still alive is one way to cope. Sometimes facing reality is too painful, and denying your loss is a temporary way to survive. In the right time, God will help you face reality and cope with your loss.

God, it doesn't feel real that my loved one is gone and won't walk through the door to tell me this is a nightmare. My pain is too raw to face that reality right now. I want to pretend this never happened. It's like I'm standing in a courtroom with the truth on one side of me and denial on the other. You are the wise, discerning Judge, and You see my pain and the truth. Help me cope with the truth. Reveal it to me today. Amen.

My Journey

_____

_____

_____

_____

_____

Part 2: Venting

YOUR JOURNEY
THROUGH VENTING

Venting: *to discharge, expel; to give expression to; to relieve pressure*

Go ahead and be angry. You do well to be angry—but don't use your anger as fuel for revenge. And don't stay angry. Don't go to bed angry. Don't give the Devil that kind of foothold in your life.
—EPHESIANS 4:26–27 THE MESSAGE

We can react with anger when we are hurt. We can strike out or use silence as a weapon to express our pain. Or we can ask God to reveal the truth behind our anger, willingly forgive others or ourselves and release it.
—KATHE WUNNENBERG

Devotion 5

JOURNEY TO THE VOLCANO OF ANGER

*"In your anger do not sin": Do not let the
sun go down while you are still angry.*

—EPHESIANS 4:26

On May 18, 1980, in southwestern Washington, a volcano that had been dormant since 1857 erupted with such violence that the mountain's top was blown off. The blast killed fifty-seven people and destroyed all life in an area the size of a large city.

When my husband and I moved to the northwest a few days after Mount St. Helens erupted, we weren't expecting any aftereffects, but ash showers were common. Gray dust sprinkled from the sky onto cars, homes, and streets. In some areas it poured down, requiring dump trucks to haul off the debris. People carried umbrellas and sported surgical masks as ash-shield attire.

Several months later, Rich and I drove to see the mountain. What had once been acres of plants, flowers, and green trees was a vast, barren area, charred and cluttered with debris. The stench of putrid gases and burned wood filled the air. We felt uneasy as we wondered, *Could this happen again?*

In our grief journey, sometimes our feelings remain dormant and inactive for weeks, months, or years. We don't realize they are building up until, without warning, something triggers them, and we blow! Our anger erupts and devastates everything and everyone in our path. The emotional blast shocks us and those around us. *Where did that come from?* we wonder. Then we realize that our journey through grief has taken us to the volcano of anger.

Jerry remembers the day he blew. A year had passed since his wife's death, and he was planning to play golf with a friend. As he was dressing, he sensed uneasiness welling up within him. When his friend arrived early and urged him to hurry, without warning Jerry picked up his golf shoes and hurled them at the freshly painted family room wall. Then he slumped to the floor and wept. *Where did that come from?* he wondered.

To this day, Jerry still is not sure, but he's convinced that something triggered his hidden anger over his loss. He felt uneasy every time he looked at the aftereffects of his eruption—the black marks on his wall. He wondered if his anger would ever flare up again.

Hidden anger can be devastating. Sooner or later, if we cork our feelings from our loss, we will blow. I'm learning to recognize the different causes of my emotions. Behind my disappointment and hurt are unmet expectations and others' insensitive comments or actions. I'm fearful when I feel uncertain, unable to trust, and anxious about change.

I have a choice to make when I discover hidden emotions: confront them, keep them current, and find peace, or continue to internalize my feelings, allow them to build, and eventually blow again. Reflecting on Jerry's eruption and the black marks on his wall reminds me that my eruptions can have lasting effects too.

Your grief journey may lead you to the volcano of anger. You may not even realize you are there until you erupt without warning. You may feel devastated, regretting what you said or did. But the good news is that God understands and is willing to transform the devastating ashes of your hidden grief into beauty. He will be your gauge, the One who puts the check in your spirit when you start to internalize your emotions and allow them to build. His truth will gently remind you not to let the sun go down on your anger. Trust Him with your hidden disappointments, hurts, and fears. Release them to Him today, and let Him calm your building volcano of anger.

> God, please forgive me for allowing my anger to erupt. I'm sorry if I hurt others. Be my gauge, and let me know when I need to confront my emotions and the underlying pain from my grief that triggers my anger. Reveal to me my hidden disappointments, hurts, and fears. I release them to You right now. Calm my volcano of anger. Amen.

My Journey

_____

_____

_____

_____

_____

_____

_____

_____

_____

_____

_____

Devotion 6

JOURNEY FROM ENVY TO TRUST

> *Who is wise and understanding among you? Let*
> *them show it by their good life, by deeds done in*
> *the humility that comes from wisdom. But if you*
> *harbor bitter envy and selfish ambition in your*
> *hearts, do not boast about it or deny the truth.*
>
> —JAMES 3:13–14

Although the Bible calls us to "rejoice with those who rejoice" and "mourn with those who mourn" (Romans 12:15), sometimes in our journey through grief, it's hard to rejoice with others. If we're really honest, we might admit that we wish things were different and that we could trade places with certain people. We may discover that we avoid them and situations where they might be because their presence is too painful and triggers our emotions.

Our reaction to others may be unpredictable and may shock us at times. For example, when a friend asked me to hold her son during a worship service, reluctantly I agreed. I felt numb and disconnected. I was afraid the simple act of holding a baby would trigger the hurt from the loss of my child. However, I made it through the church service without breaking down. An earthquake had hit my emotions, and the aftershock would come soon. Later that evening, I wasn't prepared for my explosive response. I snapped at my husband, slammed the door, and sobbed uncontrollably. I was shocked by my anger. It scared me.

As I reflected on the day's happenings, I began to think about the woman who had handed me her son. She had something I didn't. Her arms were full. Mine were empty. I longed to have a son too.

My envy had been exposed. I was allowing it to destroy my relationships with others and with the Lord. It was robbing me of the love and joy I was supposed to have for others, but it had been so camouflaged by my grief that I hadn't detected it until now. My envy had to go.

We can learn from Sarah, a fellow struggler. She has more lines of print in the Bible than any other woman, is commended as a holy woman of old (1 Peter 3:5–6), and is among God's who's who of faith in Hebrews. Wealthy, charming, and beautiful, Sarah was Abraham's wife. God promised that she would be the mother of nations.

However, Sarah endured years of barrenness. I imagine that her pain must have multiplied every time she saw a newborn baby in another woman's arms. Running low on patience, Sarah took matters into her own hands and her servant, Hagar, conceived a child with Sarah's husband. Instead of satisfying her longing for a child, Sarah's envy ignited into explosive anger toward Hagar, resulting in Hagar and her child being banished.

Sarah's envy and its outcomes eventually drove her back to God. Her grief and longing nourished the development of her relationship with God. In His timing, He fulfilled His promise to Sarah. Sarah stands as proof that God is trustworthy. She reminds us that although others will fail us, God will not. She challenges us to trust God and not envy others.

Like Sarah, we all have areas of our lives that don't meet our expectations. In our grief journey, we may be tempted to compare ourselves to others or to long for what they have. The pain of our loss can distort how we think, feel, and respond.

Who has what you want? What triggers your reaction toward them? How can you turn your envy of others into an opportunity to trust God?

God, it seems as though everywhere I look, others have what I want. They have their loved ones, and I don't. Sometimes I wish I could exchange places with _____. It hurts when I'm around _____, and it triggers the emotions of my grieving soul. Help me not to compare myself to _____. Please forgive me for my silent resentment and explosive outbursts. I'm sorry for hurting others. Fill the longing in my soul with Your comfort and self-control. Replace my envy of others with trust in You. Amen.

My Journey

_____

_____

_____

_____

_____

_____

_____

_____

Devotion 7

JOURNEY TO STILL WATER

Then they cried out to the LORD in their trouble,
and he brought them out of their distress. He
stilled the storm to a whisper; the waves of the sea
were hushed. They were glad when it grew calm,
and he guided them to their desired haven.

—PSALM 107:28–30

On the first day of summer vacation, Vicki and her son, Rew, arrived at the lake to water-ski with friends. Although this was only Rew's second time skiing, the ritual was a familiar one to Vicki. She loved the water. Some of her favorite childhood memories involved water, and she hoped to pass the legacy on to her son. Her eyes sparkled as she gazed at Rew sitting in the boat, and she anticipated the memories they would make together.

They arrived in the secluded cove late in the afternoon.

The water was calm. The conditions were perfect for skiing. Everyone took turns climbing in and out of the boat. Then Rew plopped into the water to ski.

Vicki watched her son emerge from the water and cling to the towrope behind the boat puttering slowly through the cove. She was so proud of Rew. Then, without warning, a sleek, high-powered speedboat roared into the cove. Vicki watched in helpless horror as the boat struck her son, and he disappeared beneath the water.

In that moment, Vicki's life changed forever. She replayed that scene in her mind while the divers searched for Rew. Seven days later, they recovered his body.

Vicki had already lost all the men in her life—her father, grandfathers, and uncles. She had even experienced the death of her marriage when her ex-husband left her for another woman. And now her son was gone, and her anger flared.

"Why are You punishing me, God? I don't understand how You could allow this to happen!"

During the seven years that followed her son's death, Vicki turned her anger inward and simply refused to cry. She started drinking and indulged herself with periodic spending sprees. Masking her pain, she allowed her anger to mire her in depression, anorexia, and self-pity. Again and again, Vicki replayed the question in her mind, *Why are You punishing me, God?*

Shaking a fist in anger is a common response in the journey through grief. After all, God created anger, and He doesn't expect us to ignore it. Although Vicki's anger was justifiable, she misapplied it.

Jonah was another person who took his anger out on God. When Jonah went to Nineveh, the people turned from their evil ways, and God didn't destroy the city. Jonah hated the Ninevites and responded with displeasure and anger. In essence, he pointed his finger at God, asking why. He didn't realize that four fingers were pointing back at himself. Maybe that's why God asked Jonah if he had good reason to be angry (Jonah 4:9). God wanted Jonah to examine whether he had legitimate cause for his angry feelings.

Before we express anger toward God, maybe we need to listen to His questions to us: "Is it right for you to be angry?"

Anger can manifest itself in a variety of ways: depression, eating disorders, compulsive behavior, and so forth. It may cause us to misapply our anger and blame God, ourselves, or others. We may need the help of a professional to guide us through the storms of our emotions and to help us learn to cope. And we may need to seek the Maker of our emotions to heal our hurts and calm our soul.

When Jesus invited the disciples to leave the crowd and join Him on the boat, they did. I can almost hear their laughter as they ventured out on the water that day. The conditions were perfect—not a wave in sight. Then, without warning, furious waves broke over the boat, and it was nearly engulfed. Would the disciples drown? Surely death was near. They could feel it. They could taste it.

What was Jesus doing in the midst of this disaster? Sleeping! They woke Him and said to Him, "Teacher, don't you care if we drown?" (Mark 4:38). Can you hear the terror in their voices? But if you listen closely, can you also hear the anger?

I can only imagine how they must have felt toward Jesus at this moment of crisis. Did they feel abandoned? Did they yell at Him? Did they blame Him for asking them to come on the boat in the first place? Did they have a good reason to feel angry?

As I think about the waves of emotions that can overcome us when we lose a loved one, I'm reminded of that story. In the midst of the storm, the disciples called Jesus, and He came. He awoke, rebuked the wind, and said to the waves, "Quiet! Be still!" (v. 39). Then the wind died down, and all was calm.

After several years, Vicki realized that God wasn't

punishing her, but rather He was the One who really understood her anger and fear. Seven years after Rew's death, Vicki knew she couldn't survive her journey through grief alone. Although she had attended church for most of her life, she had never established a personal relationship with Jesus Christ. She knew she needed Him. Vicki cried out to Jesus to come into her life, to forgive her for her sins, and to become her Lord and Savior. And He did.

He replaced Vicki's rage with hope. Although she had reason to be angry, she now had Someone to walk with her through her personal storms of grief and to still the waves engulfing her soul.

What about you? Do you have a good reason to feel angry? Are you handling your anger in appropriate ways, or is it raging out of control? Who can help you calm your emotions?

Lord, I don't understand why You allowed the loss of my loved one. I feel as if I have good reason to vent, but I'm not sure how to express my emotions. Forgive me for hurting myself or others. I can't do this alone. You are my Maker, and I need You to guide me safely through the waves of these emotions and direct me to people who can help me. Amen.

My Journey

Devotion 8

HIDDEN LONGINGS

All my longings lie open before you, Lord;
my sighing is not hidden from you.
—PSALM 38:9

I have a painting in my home that I've named *Hidden Longings*. A pioneer woman is standing alone in a meadow, gazing across a lake to a cabin nestled in the woods. No one else is pictured, but you can tell by the curls of smoke rising from the chimney that someone lives there. The woman appears to be stranded, unable to cross the lake.

Although I can't see her face, I've often imagined what she might look like and what she might be thinking. I've envisioned tears streaming down her face as she longs to be with the people who live just across the lake. Other times I've imagined that she has a solemn, reflective look on her face as she recalls memories with her loved ones in the cabin.

Some days I think she looks scared and anxious as she looks at the cabin across the water because it represents her future and she doesn't know how to get there from where she is. Then one day it occurred to me that the woman could be red-faced and angry about her loss.

Expectations fuel our longings. When we desire something and we don't get it, our unfulfilled expectations lead to disappointment and pain. We long for things to be different, for our loved one to be alive, for our pain to go away. Our longings spark our emotions.

My unfulfilled expectation of watching my son grow up has been a painful disappointment. I've longed for things to be different, and my longings have sparked many hidden emotions during my journey through grief. At times I've pictured myself as the woman in the picture, crying, reflecting, fretting, and, yes, venting. I've snapped at my family, slammed doors, and shouted at the top of my lungs while alone in my bedroom.

Like the woman in the picture, I realize that grief is such a solitary journey. Although I wish others could understand what I feel and could walk a portion of my grief journey for me, they can't.

During those lonely times of venting, I see myself as the woman calling out to God, the Master of the cabin.

He opens the door and walks across the lake to meet me where I am. Then He wraps His arms around me and holds me. He allows me to cast my cares on Him and release my anger. He listens. He is Jehovah-rapha to me, which means "the Lord who heals." He understands my hidden longings and my anger.

Maybe you see yourself like the woman in the picture, longing for your loved one and wishing he or she were still alive. Reflecting about your past. Anxious about the future. Or red-faced and angry. It's okay to feel any of those emotions. But you don't have to be alone. Call out to God to join you. He understands your hidden longings and your pain, and He will allow you to cast your cares and anger on Him. He will meet you where you are today. Call on Him now.

God, inside I'm red-faced and angry about my loss and the changes it has forced upon me. Please come to me now. I don't want to be alone in my pain. Help me release my hidden longings to You today. You are Jehovah-rapha, the Lord who heals. Please heal my broken heart and bind up my wounds today so I can release my anger and journey on. Amen.

My Journey

_____
_____
_____
_____
_____
_____
_____
_____
_____
_____
_____
_____
_____
_____
_____
_____
_____
_____
_____
_____
_____
_____
_____
_____
_____
_____
_____

Devotion 9

Jetty of Calm

When anxiety was great within me,
your consolation brought me joy.

—Psalm 94:19

The ocean captivates me. It is massive and mysterious yet soothing and predictable. Its waves can rage fiercely yet lap calmly against the shore. It can destroy cities and lives yet provide entertainment and food. The ocean is ever changing.

That's why we hired an experienced seaman to take us on a deep-sea fishing adventure. He understood the ocean and knew how to maneuver his boat and how to keep us safe. When we boarded the boat and began to sail through the harbor, I was amazed by how calm and smooth the water was. Then I noticed that waves were crashing against a structure extending out into the sea, so I asked the seaman about it. "It's a jetty," he said. "It protects the harbor from the ocean."

A few moments later, I discovered what he meant as we left the harbor and steered into the ocean. Our boat rocked and swayed, waves crashed, and my stomach churned. I lost my balance and fell down. I got sick. With my head tucked between my knees, I kept thinking about the smooth, calm water in the harbor, behind the jetty's protection.

Your grief journey is a bit like the ocean. Some days grief feels massive and mysterious, yet on other days, it seems calm and under control. At times you may even take precautions and seek out experts who understand grief. They know how to maneuver you safely through your ocean-swell of emotions. For even though your journey has its smooth spots, eventually you realize that the waves of your emotions are getting choppier. You begin to lash out at others. Your stomach churns. You feel sick. Your anger rages. You want to be calm again and shielded from the fury. You need a personal jetty.

When you consider the acts of kindness, encouraging cards, timely phone calls, songs that soothe, and prayers that others offer on your behalf, could it be that God has brought those people into your life as jetties to calm your grieving soul? He understands the depth of your pain, and He might use these simple acts to protect you from your raging emotions. He cares about you and will provide unexpected peace and shelter when you need it. Call on Him. Thank Him for being your shield and for the people He has provided to calm your soul. Ask Him to help you find shelter in the jetties He provides today.

God, I'm sailing through the ocean of grief. Some days the grief feels massive and mysterious. Some days I can cope and am calm. Other days my emotions are choppy and rage out of control. Help me, Lord. Soothe my soul. Allow me to find shelter in the jetties that You provide for me today. Thank You for being my shield and for providing others to encourage me. Amen.

My Journey

_____

_____

_____

_____

_____

_____

Part 3: Questioning

YOUR JOURNEY
THROUGH QUESTIONING

Questioning: *to cross-examine, doubt, dispute, examine, analyze, inquire*

The "why" of so many things
Is sometimes known only to the heart of God.
But He has promised us . . .
that at all times,
in all places,
and in all circumstances,
nothing can separate us from His love.
—AUTHOR UNKNOWN

Devotion 10

WANDERING THROUGH THE
WILDERNESS OF "WHY?"

*Then the LORD spoke to Job out of the storm. He
said: "Who is this that obscures my plans with words
without knowledge? Brace yourself like a man; I
will question you, and you shall answer me."*

—JOB 38:1–3

"Mommy, why do all our babies have to die?" My
young son's question left me speechless. How
should I respond to my brokenhearted child who had
prayed so fervently that God would give our family a baby?
Should I tell him that I didn't understand either?

The "whys" began to whirl around in my mind: *Why,
after a miscarriage, years of infertility, and adopting our son,
had I become pregnant again only to discover that our baby*

had a fatal defect and would die shortly after birth? Why did I become pregnant a third time just months after losing our infant son only to miscarry our third baby? And why must I face my son tonight, on Christmas Eve, and tell him I had just lost our fourth baby? So many whys and so few answers.

Silence pervaded the room as my son waited for my response. I grasped for the right words, but none came. At first I felt uncomfortable, not knowing how to answer his question. Then I realized that was the answer.

"Jake, I don't know. All I know is that God is there, God is good, and that's enough."

I felt relieved to finally admit, "God, I don't get it!" In that moment I came to a new understanding that circumstances don't define God's character. He is who He is, no matter what happens. He is God, and I am not. My human understanding is limited. I also realize now, after many years on my grief journey and after comforting multitudes, that God is *still* good even though I still don't understand why bad things happen to good people.

What we think about God will influence how we respond to trials in this lifetime. If we feel that Job's loss of his family, possessions, and health was something Satan slipped by God while He was busy elsewhere or that Job's loss was unavoidable, think again! If we see God as the God of the Bible—sovereign, supreme, sensitive, not allowing death and trials except by divine permission—then we can have faith that He has a purpose, even if we don't know what that purpose is.

Most of us who are grieving the loss of someone we love won't have answers to our whys. During times of questioning, I reflect on Job's life and remember that no suffering can touch a believer without having first received God's permission. I must filter my loss through the lens of His will and not my human sight.

Are you wandering through the wilderness of "Why?" God understands. He is good. He is there. Sometimes that's the only answer there is.

God, even though I don't understand why this happened and maybe never will, I still know You are trustworthy. You are good. You are in control. I may not know what the future holds, but I do know who holds the future. As I continue to wander through the wilderness of "Why?" help me trust You and not lean on my own understanding. Amen.

My Journey

_____

_____

_____

_____

_____

_____

_____

_____

_____

_____

_____

_____

_____

_____

_____

_____

_____

_____

_____

_____

_____

_____

_____

_____

_____

_____

Devotion 11

THE MYSTERY OF DEATH'S TIMING

There is a time for everything, and a season for every
activity under the heavens: a time to be born and a
time to die, a time to plant and a time to uproot, a
time to kill and a time to heal, a time to tear down
and a time to build, a time to weep and a time to
laugh, a time to mourn and a time to dance.

—ECCLESIASTES 3:1–4

*D*eath's timing is a mystery. Death intrudes into our lives and snatches away our loved one. Like a detective, we feel a desperate need to solve the case, to understand why. We sift through clues, search for evidence, and examine all of God's possible motives for seizing our loved one. Frustration fuels our investigation. We seek answers to our questions but find none.

"Why now?" we ask. Death came much too soon. It left dreams undone, life unlived, words unspoken.

We may never solve the why of "the when." Yet, like Solomon, we may need to consider that there is a time and a season for everything, and we are to savor every moment.

That's what Alice discovered one morning as she walked in her backyard seeking answers and peace. The past few weeks' events had grieved her soul deeply. As she strolled through the grass, she recalled how her grandson had died just moments after his birth. It struck her as odd that birth and death could come so close together, yet his brief life had changed hers forever. She mourned the loss of never being a granny who read to him, baked him cookies, taught him to fish, drank hot chocolate with him, or watched her daughter be a mother to him.

As Alice continued to walk, she longed for a time to heal. Then she saw a green, celery-like stem with fragile, transparent blossoms coming out of the ground. The flower hadn't been there yesterday. She remembered the previous fall planting a bulb her friend had given to her, calling it "a surprise lily."

A few days later, Alice walked again in the backyard and found the blossoms had died. Disappointed, she told her friend about the short-lived bloom only to discover that the normal life span for that type of lily was a few days.

Why would God create something so beautiful and allow it

to die so quickly? Alice wondered. Her thoughts drifted to her grandchild. She reflected on the joy she had felt over the anticipation of his birth and her disappointment over his short life. She walked over to her patio, opened her Bible, and read, "Teach us to number our days and recognize how few they are; help us to spend them as we should" (Psalm 90:12 TLB).

God's truth penetrated her soul. Although many of her questions still remained unanswered, she sensed a deeper appreciation for life—whether it was brief or long.

As it was for Alice, the timing of our loved one's death may remain a mystery, but we can treasure every moment we are given as a gift. Let's make the most of our time today and our time with our loved ones. We never know when we or they may be gone.

> Lord, Your timing is a mystery to me. I admit that I don't understand why You chose to take my loved one away when You did. I wanted to experience so many things with him (her) and say so many things. I've searched for answers to my questions, but I realize there are none in this earthly life. Your Word says there is a time and a season for everything. I'm ready for a time of joy, peace, and healing. Help me embrace the time You've given me and make the most of every moment today. Amen.

My Journey

_____

_____

_____

_____

_____

_____

_____

_____

_____

_____

_____

_____

_____

_____

_____

_____

_____

_____

_____

_____

_____

_____

_____

STRANDED ON "IF ONLY" ISLAND

"Lord," Martha said to Jesus, "if you had been
here, my brother would not have died."

—JOHN 11:21

*M*artha never gave up hope. Surely her Friend would come with His healing touch. But she watched helplessly as her brother's condition worsened. She prayed and waited, waited and prayed.

After Lazarus died and his funeral was over, I imagine that Martha felt numb, body and soul, as though she, rather than her brother, had just been laid to rest in the grave. Perhaps she felt isolated and abandoned, as if she were consigned to an island in the sea with no one to rescue her.

Then, when Martha heard that Jesus had finally come, she went out to meet Him. Maybe she recalled the laughter and conversation they had shared along this path. But this homecoming was different. Her brother, Lazarus, was dead. I wonder if Martha's red, puffy eyes were filled with hurt and disappointment as she looked into His eyes and said, "Lord, . . . if you had been here, my brother would not have died. But I know that even now God will give you whatever you ask" (John 11:21–22).

Did hope sparkle in Martha's eyes when Jesus shared that her brother would rise again? She was accustomed to extraordinary things happening when He was around. But did she anticipate what Jesus would do that day? Martha watched Jesus weep. Was she surprised by His tears? Did she hand Him a tissue to comfort Him? When she followed Him to Lazarus's tomb, was she cautiously hopeful or was she still consumed by the thought, *If only You had been here*?

Like Martha lamented, maybe you've said, "Lord, if only You had been here, my loved one wouldn't have died." Someone you loved was facing death, and you cried out to Jesus for help. You prayed. You waited. You claimed His promises. But still, the loved one died. Perhaps you've had regrets about how events unfolded. You've thought, *If only I had prayed harder . . . If only I had encouraged him to go to the doctor sooner . . . If only the accident had never occurred . . . If only the Lord had come and saved him.*

If only . . . if only . . . if only.

"If only" thinking can destroy us emotionally and spiritually. Too often we equate God's healing with His presence and death with His absence. When a loved one dies, we feel abandoned or even punished. Such conclusions can make us feel hopeless and angry, resentful and bitter. We blame instead of believe. And then we end up on "if only" island.

If you feel stranded on your own "if only" island, imagine for a moment that you notice a ship in the distance. It sails closer, and then Jesus steps ashore to greet you. You stomp over to confront Him with your questions, but He answers only with His tears. Only with His embrace. He understands what it feels like to cry out and not to be rescued. He knows how it feels to be deserted and abandoned. In His own body, He has experienced the pain of death.

As He reaches out His hands to you, you notice the nail marks. You hear Him say, *If only you would come to Me, I would give you rest. If only you would believe that I am always with you. If only you would cast all your cares on Me because I care for you. If only you would let go of your "if onlys" and trust Me with all your heart.*

Yes, if only.

Lord, death is so difficult and so confusing. There's so much I don't understand. But You understand. I'm tired of blaming You for not coming to the rescue. I don't want to entertain "if only" thinking anymore. Please replace my blaming with believing. Help me surrender my questions and cares. Bring me back from my lonely island of questioning and anger, and restore my hope. Amen.

My Journey

FROM TRAGEDY TO TRIUMPH

Now I want you to know, brothers and
sisters, that what has happened to me has
actually served to advance the gospel.

—PHILIPPIANS 1:12

One Christmas Eve, Karen walked up the old farmhouse's creaky steps. Deciding to move to the country and to enjoy a simpler lifestyle was a gift both she and her husband were glad they had decided to give their family. In just a few short months, surrounded by pigs and chickens, they had made a lifetime of memories.

Karen tiptoed down the hall to the bedroom where her daughters were sleeping. She bent down and gently kissed their foreheads. She could hardly wait to see their beaming faces on Christmas morning as they opened their gifts beneath the tree.

Moments later, Karen cuddled next to her husband and drifted off to sleep. Her dreams turned to nightmares when she and Willie awoke to a crackling noise. As they descended the stairs, they saw flames everywhere. *I have to get the girls*, Karen thought. She raced up the steps toward their room, but she couldn't penetrate the dense, black fog pouring out of the doorway. "Rachel, Ruthie, get up!" she screamed. But there was no response.

Willie bolted through the darkness toward the girls' room. Karen knew he would come running out with the girls. But Willie didn't return. The intense heat was burning Karen's skin and hair as she gasped for air. There was no escape. *Help me, God! Should I stay or should I go?* Then she remembered the ladder in her bedroom for emergencies. She crashed through the window and climbed down to safety.

By this time, the fire was raging out of control. Karen was numb with disbelief, and the emptiness she felt was beyond description. Her entire family was gone. She questioned why this tragedy had happened and how she would survive beyond it.

If we look at circumstances from a human point of view, we have good reason to question and despair. We don't understand the big picture and why God allowed something so terrible to happen.

Jesus Himself asked the question, "My God, my God, why have you forsaken me?" (Matthew 27:46) when He was dying on the cross. By doing so, He gave us permission to cry out to God in our grief.

From a human point of view, Jesus' death was a tragedy. Yet what looked like a devastating setback was, in spiritual reality, a turning point in history. In the same way, God can transform our questions, suffering, and circumstances into a gift to help others who are doubting God. This book is a tangible reminder of how God has transformed my hurt into hope and my pain into purpose.

Tragedies can result in modern-day triumphs. That's what happened when a beautiful, vibrant, athletic young woman had an accident that permanently paralyzed her from the neck down. "Terrible," we say. And we're right. "Her life is ruined," we decide. And we're wrong! Through that accident, Joni Eareckson Tada became a great gift to the church and found a new and fulfilling life for herself to spread hope to others. Tragedy became triumph.

My friends Arie and Shayla lost their twins prematurely and started a nonprofit ministry distributing boxes of hope to grieving families in the hospital. My book *Grieving the Child I Never Knew* is included in their boxes.

After a season of grieving the loss of her family, Karen

met a compassionate man, remarried, and had twins. Although her new family would never replace the family she had lost and her questions remained unanswered, she didn't turn away from her pain but instead turned to God. Karen began to share her story through musical concerts to give hope to the hurting.

When tragedies strike (and they will), the apostle Paul urged us in Philippians 1:12 to look past the circumstances. What seems like defeat may turn into victory, what looks like suffering may become joy, and what appears to be a tragedy may lead to spiritual triumph.

Lord, thank You for Your patience with me and for giving me permission to ask why, just as Jesus did. Fill my mind with Your perspective, and make my loss and suffering count for something good that will help others who are questioning. Amen.

My Journey

_____

_____

_____

_____

_____

_____

_____

_____

_____

_____

_____

_____

_____

_____

_____

_____

_____

_____

_____

_____

_____

_____

_____

_____

_____

_____

Part 4: Bargaining

Your Journey
Through Bargaining

Bargaining: *to negotiate, haggle; to come to terms; to agree, barter*

Trust in the Lord with all your heart and lean not on your own understanding; in all your ways submit to him, and he will make your paths straight.
—Proverbs 3:5–6

"For I know the plans I have for you," declares the Lord, "plans to prosper you and not to harm you, plans to give you hope and a future."
—Jeremiah 29:11

Devotion 14

JOURNEY TO THE
MARKETPLACE OF BARGAINING

For I can do everything through Christ,
who gives me strength.
—PHILIPPIANS 4:13 NLT

I grew up in a family of small-business owners. My grandfather owned the town's general store, my uncle June was the postmaster, my dad owned the gas station, my mom owned the beauty parlor, and my uncle Bob owned the funeral home. I believed our family could do everything. All we needed was a preacher in the family and our slogan could be, "We can do it all . . . from marry to bury." From this rural beginning, I learned the necessity of good customer service and the importance of bargaining—developing techniques and incentives to entice people to buy.

Sales and marketing was a natural career path for me, and I thrived during the many years I spent in media advertising sales. Problem solving and negotiating were my specialties.

When my sales manager proposed a sales contest with a trip to San Francisco as a prize, I was determined to win. I strategically planned how to make my presentation and ways to overcome any possible objections a client might have. I strolled into my first client's office the next day and shared the opportunity. He wasn't convinced. I rebutted his objections. I was about to give up when I remembered an additional incentive I thought I could talk my boss into giving. It worked! He bought it.

The only hurdle was to convince my sales manager to accept my conditions. Unfortunately, she rejected my proposal. I was disappointed at the time, but looking back, I'm glad she did because my client ended up going out of business. His failure would have cost me the trip (which I ended up winning anyway) as well as my commission.

Sometimes in our journey through grief we think we know it all and persist in negotiating with God about our loss. Like a bargaining salesperson, we employ sales techniques and propose incentives to God to sweeten the deal—or at least to lessen the pain. We rebut His objections and go for the close, but often He rejects our proposal. We may feel disappointed, even angry. Yet He sees beyond our short-term request. He understands the overall plan and has a reason for saying no to us. Over time we may start to understand, but even if we don't, God does. When we exchange our *I can do it all* thinking for *I can do all things through Christ who strengthens me* thinking, we are well on our way to moving forward in our journey through grief.

God, sometimes I propose solutions, negotiate, and even offer You incentives to accept my terms, but often You reject them. Please forgive me for being disappointed and angry with You. Help me accept Your answers even though I may not understand them. You are the God who sees the future. Be my strength. Help me today to trust You with my loss. Amen.

My Journey

_____

_____

_____

_____

_____

FATHER KNOWS BEST

Even though I walk through the darkest valley,
I will fear no evil, for you are with me; your
rod and your staff, they comfort me.

—PSALM 23:4

When King Hezekiah discovered he was about to die, his grief drove him through the gates of bargaining. He prayed to God and reminded Him of his faithfulness and good deeds. He wept bitterly as he faced death. Hezekiah obviously didn't agree with God's decision and bargained for a different outcome. In this situation, God did grant Hezekiah's request and extended his life. However, there's more to the story than meets the eye.

God added fifteen years to Hezekiah's life, but during that time Manasseh, his son, was born. Manasseh became the most wicked king in Israel's history. Yes, God granted

Hezekiah's request, but it might have been better if He hadn't!

Grief may drive us to bargain with God. Sharing honest feelings with God is healthy, and He wants us to cast our hurts and cares on Him. But when we're tempted to tell Him how to do His job, we might want to stop and remember Hezekiah. Rather than plead for our way, perhaps we should simply say, "God, only if it's for the best." We don't see the future, but God does. He is all knowing and sovereign. Even though we may not understand, He is our Father, and He knows best.

God, sometimes I wish I could change the outcome of my circumstances. I want to be in control. Please forgive me for telling You how to do Your job. Even though I don't understand, I know You must have a reason. Help me trust You. I release my fear, uncertainty, and conditions to You today. Grant my desire only if it's for the best. Amen.

My Journey

_____

_____

_____

_____

_____

_____

_____

_____

_____

_____

_____

_____

_____

_____

_____

_____

_____

_____

_____

_____

_____

_____

_____

_____

God Delivered More
Than I Bargained For

Now to him who is able to do immeasurably more than all
we ask or imagine, according to his power that is at work
within us, to him be glory in the church and in Christ Jesus
throughout all generations, for ever and ever! Amen.
—Ephesians 3:20–21

*K*ath, I've been in a car accident. I'm in the emergency room in Baltimore."

My heart froze. "Rich, what happened?"

"I was knocked unconscious and brought here by helicopter. Kath, they had to cut off my new suit . . ." My husband's voice cracked as he fought back tears.

I tightly clutched the receiver. *I should be there with him right now, not two thousand miles away in Phoenix.* I felt helpless, yet I knew I needed to be strong. I soothed him with words. I prayed with him over the phone that God would be his Peace, Protector, and Comforter and that He would take care of every detail of this situation . . . including getting me there.

"Good-bye, Kath," were Rich's final words in our conversation. I replayed them in my mind and wondered if these would be his last. *God, You've already taken my son. Please don't take my husband too*, I pleaded. I relived my fear and anguish when I had begged God to spare my son. I knew God was capable of sparing him, but He had chosen not to in spite of my bargaining. Would I have to endure another loss just six months later?

Only God knew.

At that moment all I knew was that I had to trust God, even though I wanted to tell Him how to do His job. My husband was in His hands.

Then I watched as God worked out every detail. Relief enveloped me when I walked into the intensive care unit and heard Rich say, "Hello." His nurse assured me that he would recover from his broken ribs, bruises, and concussion.

Two days later, Rich was released from the hospital, and his company's special treatment overwhelmed us. A coworker transported us to a plush hotel. Wheelchair service whisked us to our hotel suite, and we enjoyed room service between naps. When the chef came to our room to personally serve our food and to inquire about Rich, we wondered what God would do next.

Well, the first-class seats and a nonstop flight home to Phoenix minimized Rich's pain. Then I picked up our son and discovered that my friend had laundered his clothes and even purchased his next day's school supplies. God cared about every detail!

Just when I thought God was finished, He surprised us again. All expenses incurred for this trip, including the new suit the hospital attendants had cut off Rich, would be covered by his company. God even provided a souvenir from this experience—a two-inch remnant of blue fabric— which, as far as we know, is the only remnant of Rich's suit.

We've kept that remnant to encourage us during times of uncertainty in our grief journey, to remind us that God is faithful. He may not always answer our requests in the way we desire, but when we trust Him with the details, He will give us more than we bargained for.

Pleading and bargaining with God are such normal parts of the grief journey. Yet your bargain may not be one God can accept. You may even be tempted to think

God hasn't heard your pleas. But remember the cross for a moment, and you'll realize that Jesus didn't bargain with God. Instead He surrendered Himself in unconditional love. And you reaped the benefits. God gave you much more than you bargained for.

> God, sometimes You answer my prayers differently than I asked You to. My conditions aren't always part of Your plans. I don't understand Your ways, and I don't want to endure pain and loss. Help me trust You with the details of my life. Replace my conditions with Your unconditional love. Thank You for sacrificing Your life for me and for giving me more than I bargained for—eternal hope. Show me how to trust You today. Amen.

My Journey

_____

_____

_____

_____

_____

_____

Bargaining About Your Loved One's Eternal Future

For it is by grace you have been saved, through faith—and this is not from yourselves, it is the gift of God—not by works, so that no one can boast.
—Ephesians 2:8–9

"For God so loved the world that he gave his one and only Son, that whoever believes in him shall not perish but have eternal life."
—John 3:16

We all want to believe our loved ones are in heaven. It comforts us and brings closure to our grief knowing that someday we will see them again. But all too often I've observed well-meaning pastors, family, and friends speaking about a person's heavenly future without knowing for certain whether it's true.

How do we know if our loved one is in heaven? Can we make that judgment? And how do we cope with the uncertainty of not knowing?

Picturing our loved ones anywhere besides heaven is distressing. Dealing with their deaths is painful enough, but living with the uncertainty of their eternal future can overwhelm us. To cope, we may find ourselves bargaining with others and with God about our loved one's eternal future. "But she was a good person"; "He went to church and was always helping others"; "Even though she didn't talk about God, I'm sure she must have loved Him"; "If God is a loving God, then He wouldn't turn His back on my loved one." We desperately grasp for certainty to end our turmoil. We want to wrap up our loved one's life in bright paper like a present, tape it together with good works and justifications, and top it off with a bow of certainty—an eternal life with God.

I wonder if that's what James and John's mother was thinking when she approached Jesus and bargained with Him about her sons' eternal positions. She must have wanted to do everything within her power to put a bow on their future, even if it meant pleading and negotiating.

How discouraged she must have felt when Jesus responded, "You don't know what you are asking . . . Can you drink the cup I am going to drink? . . . You will indeed drink from my cup, but to sit at my right or left is not for me to grant. These places belong to those for whom they have been prepared by my Father" (Matthew 20:22–23).

We cannot secure another person's place in heaven or his or her eternal future, regardless of how hard we plead, justify, or bargain with God. Some things, like our loved one's eternal future after they die, are out of our control.

Yet, amid this uncertainty we can cling to an eternal God who is merciful beyond our understanding. His Word promises that eternal life is a free gift of grace, and if you confess with your mouth "Jesus is Lord" and believe in your heart that God raised Him from the dead, you will be saved (Romans 10:9). Could this have happened on your loved one's deathbed or in a supernatural way? Absolutely. With God, all things are possible. His desire is that no one would perish. Will you see your loved one in heaven? Only God knows. But more important, will *you* spend eternity with God? That free gift is waiting for you to reject or receive. Put the bow of certainty on your eternal future today.

Lord, I commit my uncertainty about my loved one's eternal future to You today. God, thank You for being merciful. I want to know with certainty that I will spend eternity with You. I believe You so loved the world that You gave Your one and only Son, Jesus, to die on the cross for my sins. He conquered death, rose again, and is preparing a place in heaven for me to live eternally with Him. Come into my life today. Be my Lord and Savior. I want to live eternally with You. Amen.

My Journey

_____

_____

_____

_____

_____

_____

_____

_____

_____

_____

_____

Part 5: Crying

YOUR JOURNEY THROUGH CRYING

Crying: *an utterance of distress, rage, or pain; sobbing, weeping, releasing tears*

When our heart is breaking and we cannot speak, tears become our prayers that express our heart to God.
—KATHE WUNNENBERG

Weeping may stay for the night, but rejoicing comes in the morning.
—PSALM 30:5

"He will wipe every tear from their eyes. There will be no more death or mourning or crying or pain, for the old order of things has passed away."
—REVELATION 21:4

Devotion 18

FACING THE FLASH
FLOODS OF TEARS

Record my misery; list my tears on your
scroll—are they not in your record?
—PSALM 56:8

When too much pressure is put on the heart, tears are its safety valve. No matter how hard we try to control ourselves, sometimes there's just no stopping tears. Though we may try to sandbag our emotions, sooner or later the wall breaks and the tears come flooding through.

They may erupt when we hear a favorite song, smell a familiar cologne, or see a family picture and remember how much we miss our loved one. Tears are unpredictable. They may surface in the middle of the night, in the middle of the grocery store, or in the middle of a conversation. Sometimes they come for no apparent reason at all.

One "flash flood" occurred for me at an out-of-state conference. Fifteen of us had gathered in the living room of a turn-of-the-century mansion for our closing session. Though we had been strangers when we had arrived just days earlier, I realized by the constant buzz of conversation that friendships had already been kindled. When the leader signaled it was time to begin, I noticed she had placed a large, antique chair in the middle of the room. One by one, she asked each of us to take our turn sitting in the chair while the rest of us showered that person with encouraging words and prayer.

When my turn came, I sat down and looked at the caring eyes that surrounded me. Something about this felt familiar. Immediately I began to weep.

Why was I reacting this way? Then it hit me. The last time I had sat in a circle like this had been a month before my baby's death. My friends had gathered to give me an "encouragement shower" to help me face my baby's birth and impending death. My flashback triggered a flash flood.

That's the mystery of grief; it's personal and unique. No two people grieve exactly the same way. But most (if not all) will say that the journey through the valley of tears is normal and necessary. So grab a tissue (or a box or two), and allow your tears to relieve the pressure from your hurting heart.

Lord, I'm crying again. Will my tears ever stop? Your ledger for my tears must be overflowing. Because You created tears and You wept when Your friend Lazarus died, I know it's okay to cry. You know my heart is breaking, and You understand my pain. Please comfort me today and help me trust You through the flash flood of tears. Amen.

My Journey

_____

_____

_____

_____

_____

_____

_____

_____

_____

Devotion 19

HAPPY-SAD TEARS

*"Whenever I bring clouds over the earth and the rainbow
appears in the clouds, I will remember my covenant between
me and you and all living creatures of every kind. Never
again will the waters become a flood to destroy all life."*

—GENESIS 9:14–15

The day of the anniversary of my son's death is a time
I look forward to yet dread. Each year it's a milestone
to celebrate—I have survived another year without my son.

One year early in my grief journey, in anticipation of
the day, I prepared myself for a flurry of emotions and
made sure I had plenty of tissues. I carefully planned a
memorable day that included a trip to the cemetery, a service project in honor of my son, and time alone to reflect.

I gave myself permission to cry whenever I felt like it,
to think about my son, and to talk about him with others.

How old would he be now? What would he be doing? What would he look like? What would his favorite book or movie be? What would his laugh sound like? How would his hug feel? How would he and his big brother get along?

I continued to ponder. *What had he learned in heaven? What was it like to be in God's presence with no pain, darkness, or tears? Whom did he spend time with there?*

I felt a tear trickle down my cheek just as my son, Jake, walked into the room. He gave me a long, questioning stare. "Mom, why are crying and smiling at the same time?"

Without thinking, I said, "These are happy-sad tears."

"Happy-sad tears? What do you mean, Mom?"

"Well, I'm happy because your brother is in heaven, but I'm sad because I miss him today."

Jake nodded, handed me a tissue, and gave me a reassuring hug. Amazingly, this seven-year-old boy understood and gave me permission to cry.

Later that week Jake ran into the house and screamed, "Mom, come quick!"

Fearing the worst, I bolted outside, only to discover him standing in the middle of the yard, smiling as it rained. Just as I was about to ground him for scaring me, he pointed to the sky. The sun was shining through the clouds, and a rainbow was beginning to appear.

"Mom, I've never seen it rain and shine at the same time. It reminds me of happy-sad tears."

I nodded, smiled, and walked over to stand in the rain with him. I felt affirmed that tears and smiles can happen at the same time in our grief journey. Maybe it's time for you to embrace your tears and smile as you journey on.

Lord, today is another milestone for me without my loved one—I've made it through another day, another week, another month. Help me remember and celebrate his (her) life. Some of my memories make me smile and cry at the same time. Help me to see Your sunshine in the midst of my tears and to have eyes to see the rainbow through my grief. Amen.

My Journey

_____

_____

_____

_____

_____

_____

"Remembering" Tears

"The LORD does not look at the things people look at. People look at the outward appearance, but the LORD looks at the heart."

—1 SAMUEL 16:7

Have you ever considered something to be trash only to discover it was a priceless treasure to someone else?

During a spring-cleaning frenzy, I determined to give away or throw away anything we didn't use. When I came to our bedroom, I decided I would surprise my husband and clean out his dresser drawers. As I sorted through his belongings, I quickly discovered that a lot of his things were outdated, in need of repair, or too small.

"What are these?" I chuckled as I picked up a tattered pair of black leather gloves held together by tape. "He can't wear these. I'll buy him a new pair." I tossed them onto the trash pile and continued my cleaning task.

"What on earth are you doing, Kath?" my husband asked as he maneuvered through piles on the floor.

"Surprise! I'm cleaning and getting rid of the junk," I announced.

"You're not throwing away any of my things, are you?"

I nodded and pointed to the trash pile.

He plopped down on the floor and began to examine each item. Then he picked up the black leather gloves. He cradled them gently in his hands as if he held a priceless jewel, staring at them for a long time. When he looked at me, his eyes were tear filled. "These were my dad's."

I froze. I didn't know what to say.

Rich recalled memories of helping his dad with carpentry projects, climbing on the roof with him, and sitting with him in the back of the church.

What a relationship they built in only eight short years, I thought as tears rolled down my cheeks. How sad that I almost trashed something so precious to Rich. Our journey through grief may not always be understood. Items or memories that appear insignificant and "trash-worthy" to others may be priceless treasures to us. Never underestimate what may trigger your "remembering" tears.

Well-meaning family and friends may think they are helping you get through your loss by removing items from your sight or by unknowingly trashing your treasures. But God is the God of remembrance. He values what was. He understands your loss, your pain, your tears, and your treasure. Trust Him with the memories of your loved one. Tell Him today.

God, I'm crying again, but today my tears are "remembering" tears. Thank You for giving me memories of my loved one. Thank You for the mementos that trigger memories of a special time. Please help me forgive the people who have been insensitive to me. They mean well, but they don't understand that what is insignificant to them is priceless to me. You are my God of remembrance. Thank You for understanding and for seeing beyond appearances and looking into my heart. I trust You with my memories. Amen.

My Journey

_____

_____

_____

_____

_____

OTHERS' TEARS

*Rejoice with those who rejoice; mourn
with those who mourn.*

—ROMANS 12:15

Too often in our journey through grief we forget that others are affected by the loss of our loved one and are suffering too. Family members, young children, coworkers, neighbors, and friends feel deeply, but often we overlook or minimize their pain because we're so absorbed by our own grief. Others may grieve differently than we do, but they still grieve. At times they might even conceal their tears to protect us from their pain.

I realized this when my friend Jan came to see me a few months after my son's death. Her frequent hugs, acts of kindness, and uplifting attitude were a constant source of encouragement to me during my dark times of sadness and grief, but I never stopped to consider how my son's death had affected her until that day.

Jan's face was somber as she sat down. When I asked her about it, she hesitated. "Kathe, I've been trying to be so strong for you. It never occurred to me I haven't allowed myself to grieve." Jan's lip trembled as a tear trickled down her cheek.

I listened as she shared how my son's death had touched her and about her reluctance to tell me since I was enduring my own pain. At that moment, I realized that loss impacts others, and I needed to give them permission to grieve. Jan and I embraced and cried together.

As you journey through grief, you may encounter others' tears. At times you may need to look beyond your own pain and be sensitive to how others are concealing their grief from you. Hidden grief may be disguised in a spouse's silence, a child's misbehavior, or a family member's avoidance or upbeat mood. Remember, you aren't the only one grieving the loss of a loved one. Others may need you to give them permission to share their pain.

Lord, thank You for those who have encouraged me through my loss. Their compassion and sensitivity have strengthened me. Forgive me for the times I've been absorbed by my grief and haven't realized how my loss has affected others. Open my eyes to their hidden grief. Reveal to me who these people are today. Help me to approach them and to comfort them in their grief journeys. Amen.

My Journey

Devotion 22

Growing Tears

*I waited patiently for God to help me; then he listened
and heard my cry. He lifted me out of the pit of despair,
out from the bog and the mire, and set my feet on a
hard, firm path, and steadied me as I walked along.*
—Psalm 40:1–2 TLB

As a child, I used to visit my grandparents' home in
the country, where they relied on a cistern to water
their garden. The cistern was an artificial reservoir, a rock-
like well beneath the ground for storing rainwater. When
the autumn rains came, water rushed down the gutters on
my grandparents' home and filled the cistern. Then, during the spring, the water would release to nourish sprouting
plants. By summer, my grandparents' garden was green
and lush, a result of the cistern's life-giving water.

During some seasons in our journey through grief, our

reservoir stores up tears, and during other seasons, those tears flow. When we release them, they wash away our anger, guilt, and unforgiveness and water our soul's garden. We feel refreshed and relieved. The seeds of new beginnings and new possibilities begin to take root and emerge from our soul's soil. Tears can nourish us and help us grow through our grief. Over time we may see a lush, green garden of hope, and our soul might bloom with the strength to press on—a result of God's life-giving power through our tears.

Don't deny yourself or others the opportunity to cry. Too often well-meaning people pat a grieving person on the arm and say, "Oh, don't cry. You'll get through this."

I used to say that to people. Was I uncaring or uncomfortable? No, I believed my words were encouraging. I didn't understand how hurtful they were until I was the receiver of those "comforting" words after my son's death.

Then I realized that storing up my tears wouldn't remove my pain. It only added more emotional debris to my reservoir. I'll never forget the sense of relief I felt when a friend said, "Weep with all your heart. Tears will water and grow your soul." How comforting to have another person recognize that tears are a growing part of my journey through grief.

Maybe that's why Jesus wept after Lazarus died and why Jesus never condemned others for crying, thereby giving us permission to cry as well. Like a cistern, at times our reservoir is full, and we need to release our tears. Give yourself permission to cry. Allow God's power to use your tears to refresh you and transform your soul into a lush garden.

God, crying makes me feel weak and out of control. I don't want others to feel uncomfortable or at a loss for words when I cry, but I do want to be strong again. I know that You wept when You lost loved ones and that You never condemned others for crying. Yet I struggle to give myself permission to cry. Reach down into the cistern of my soul and help me release my fears and tears to You. Wash away my anger, guilt, and unforgiveness. Transform me. Use my tears to water my emerging hopes. Grow my soul into a blooming garden. Amen.

My Journey

_____

_____

_____

_____

_____

Part 6: Surrendering

Your Journey
Through Surrendering

Surrendering*: to yield to the power, control, or possession of; to give up completely; to give oneself over to something; to relinquish*

If we will only surrender ourselves utterly to the Lord and will trust Him perfectly, we shall find our souls "mounting up with wings as eagles" to the "heavenly places" in Christ Jesus where earthly annoyances or sorrows have no power to disturb us.
—Hannah Whitall Smith

"Father, if you are willing, take this cup from me; yet not my will, but yours be done."
—Luke 22:42

Devotion 23

JOURNEY INTO THE
FIRE OF SURRENDER

*For he will be like a refiner's fire or a launderer's soap.
He will sit as a refiner and purifier of silver; he will
purify the Levites and refine them like gold and silver.*

—MALACHI 3:2–3

The embers glowed as the blacksmith stoked the fire. One callused hand held a piece of metal to the anvil while the other clasped a hammer. Then he thrust the metal into the fire and pounded. *Clang. Thud. Clang.* In the fire, the metal was transformed. The duet of the fire and the hammer continued until the blacksmith's work was finally complete—a masterpiece, a tool.

Loss transforms us, reshaping and redefining who we are. Yet the refining process isn't anything easy. Sometimes it creates terrible pain and discomfort as you place yourself in the divine Blacksmith's hands. He pounds His hammer on your anger, then your fears. Another crushing blow upon your blaming and your tears. You're relieved that it's finished, but then you feel the heat. You try to escape, but your fight is futile. Finally you yield to the fire of surrender. The flames melt your pride, guilt, doubt, resentment, and unforgiveness. *There's nothing left to melt or pound*, you think. You're in the process of being transformed into a masterpiece in the divine Blacksmith's hand.

Our journey into the fire of surrender may happen all at once or at numerous times throughout the different seasons of grief. When we choose to surrender our grief, God can and will transform it. Our fear becomes faith. Our doubt becomes trust. Our hurt becomes hope. God can reshape *us* too. Rather than adopting the identity of widower or childless parent, we can let God help us forge a new identity as a comforter, advocate, supporter group leader, or hopelifter to help others.

Should you decide to enter the fire of surrender and start the process of reshaping, remember that God is the master Refiner. He will transform you and your loss into a productive masterpiece.

God, my loss has transformed me. I'm not who I used to be, but I'm confused about who I need to become. I'm afraid to change and move forward in my journey of grief. Is now the right time for me? I don't want to resist Your transforming power. Help me yield my loss and my potential to You today. I will enter the fire of surrender and allow You to pound and refine me. You are the master Refiner who can remove all the impurities of my grief. Transform my loss and my being into a productive masterpiece that You can use. Amen.

My Journey

_____

_____

_____

_____

_____

_____

_____

_____

_____

_____

RUNNING FROM GOD

> *"Call on me in the day of trouble; I will*
> *deliver you, and you will honor me."*
>
> —PSALM 50:15

At times in my grief journey I've resisted God's guidance and direction. My expectations, emotions, or will usually led me astray. But in spite of my failings and shortcomings, God has always been gracious. Amazingly, He works through me anyway—though, looking back, I wonder how much more of an impact I might have made if I had surrendered to Him instead of running from Him.

Jonah's story gives me hope. He was about as far out of fellowship with God as a believer can get. He was running away from Him when that terrifying storm hit the ship he was on, frightening all aboard. Then Jonah confessed his responsibility and convinced the sailors to throw him overboard. Imagine the look of surprise on their sea-soaked faces when they tossed Jonah overboard and the storm stopped. This convinced them of the power of Jonah's God, and they offered a sacrifice to the Lord and made vows to Him. Ironically, God used runaway Jonah to introduce Himself to a shipload of sailors. Unfortunately, Jonah missed out on the celebration and the blessing of seeing his sailing companions experience God as he sank deeper into the sea.

Like Jonah, we may feel as if we are sinking from the burden of our grief. We feel discouraged and distant from God. We begin to think that our grief is our weight to carry and not His. We resist His help, and then we run away. We fool ourselves into believing that we can deal with our sea of personal troubles, sorrows, and consequences. And we may for a while. We may even sense that we are being used to help others. But, in time, the waves of our independence become so turbulent that they begin affecting others around us. Then we must throw ourselves on God's mercy, believing that He is waiting to save us from our sea of sorrow. Surrendering our grief doesn't mean that we agree with or understand what God plans, but rather we acknowledge that He knows best and are willing to obey Him anyway.

Surrendering my will, my hurts, and my hopes to God is a daily journey for me. I may still want to run, but that's when God reminds me of Jonah. When Jonah was running from the Lord, God used him to touch a shipload of people. But when Jonah surrendered his life to God, He used him to change an entire city.

Where are you in your relationship with God? In close fellowship with Him, or running from Him because you don't understand His purposes? Or running because you *do* understand His purposes and don't like them? You cannot escape God. He will pursue you just as He pursued Jonah. Whatever your doubts, pain, anger, or disobedience, God is willing to accept those who call on Him for help. Our past failings don't disqualify us from joining God in the great purposes He is working out through our grief even now. What motivation for us to surrender to Him and to be committed fully to do His will. Let's not settle for touching a shipload of lives, but rather let us allow God to use our grief to transform many!

God, I feel disconnected and distant from You. I've allowed my emotions, expectations, and will to lead me astray. I've been running from You. I've resisted Your help and have been trying to carry my burden of grief alone. I'm drowning in discouragement and sorrow. I give up. I'm sorry for running away from You. Please help me throw myself at Your mercy. Save me from my sea of sorrow. I surrender my failings, doubt, pain, anger, and grief to You today. Amen.

My Journey

_____

_____

_____

_____

_____

_____

_____

_____

_____

_____

_____

Devotion 25

REQUIRED COURSES

May the Lord answer you when you are in distress; may the name of the God of Jacob protect you. May he send you help from the sanctuary and grant you support from Zion.

—Psalm 20:1–2

*M*y college diploma reminds me of times when I sat in my advisor's office seeking direction about how to earn my degree and what courses I needed to take. Some courses seemed illogical, yet I suffered through them because I had to in order to reach my goal. Of course, had I been empowered to design the curriculum, I would have chosen electives that required minimal effort.

Our grief journey may feel like being in school again, striving to graduate. We may find ourselves in required courses, such as "Living with Loneliness," "Coping with Change," or "Managing Emotions." They are a mandatory part of our grief curriculum. At times we may feel as if we're flunking, with no hope of graduating from our grief; at other times we may feel as if we've passed a basic course, only to discover that we're required to take a higher-level class and learn new aspects about grieving.

As a fellow student in the school of grieving, I've come to realize that my required courses may look different from yours, yet we probably share the same desired outcome: to pass the classes and journey successfully through grief. Numerous times I've been tempted to drop out and wallow in self-pity and bitterness. Although I wanted to succeed, no amount of studying, knowledge, or tutoring was enough to help me pass. I always fell short. That's when I finally gave up trying to move forward in my own strength. Surrendering my pain, my loss, and my required courses to God enabled me to persevere.

Although I still haven't graduated from the school of grieving, I know that each required course brings me one step closer and that my divine Advisor is available to encourage me and to remind me to surrender each course to Him.

When I reflect on David's life in 1 and 2 Samuel, I'm reminded of his required courses: "Obedience"; "Success"; "Overcoming Lust, Lying, and Murder"; and "Losing a Son." David understood the outcome of relying on his own strength. He failed many courses, yet his pain and anguish led him to surrender to God.

What about you? Which of grief's required courses are you enrolled in? Are you relying on your own strength, or are you ready to surrender your pain and loss to God and to trust His strength to help you through? He is ready to be your Advisor, to help you journey through grief successfully. Why not let go and let God help?

God, whether I like it or not, I'm a student in the school of grief, and I can learn from You during this time. You know just how tough my courses are and that I often feel as if I'm in over my head. Please help me surrender my grief to You today. Be my divine Advisor and encourage me to persevere. Amen.

My Journey

_____

_____

_____

_____

_____

Devotion 26

RECEIVING A LIFT IS A GIFT

Therefore encourage one another and build each other up.
—1 THESSALONIANS 5:11

Who lifts you up through your letdowns? Who has tried to support you, though you've refused their help?

Allowing others to encourage us can make us feel uneasy. Somehow it seems easier to give than to receive. If this is true of you, you may be missing out on a healing part of the journey through grief.

Remember the story of the paralytic in Mark 2? Imagine, for a moment, how he must have felt, unable to live life as a healthy man. I wonder if tears filled his eyes when he dreamed about the life he longed for. Did he feel lonely, afraid, and misunderstood? When others tried to help, did his anger flare because he didn't want to appear needy?

Perhaps when his four friends came to see him, he was surprised his friends were still speaking to him after his insistence that they leave him alone. Did he feel undeserving of these persistent friends?

When they gathered around him and told him they were taking him to see Jesus, did he try to discourage them? Perhaps one of his friends bathed him, dressed him, combed his hair. Did he feel self-conscious or humbled by the outpouring of his friends' love demonstrated in such a practical way? When his friends placed him on the mat, picked it up, and carried him through the streets, did he enjoy the fresh air and join in with their singing and laughter? Was he overwhelmed or disappointed when they arrived in front of the house overflowing with people? As he lay there, did he thank his friends for trying and encourage them to take him home? When they forged up the outdoor steps carrying him on his mat to the roof, I wonder if he were afraid. As his friends dug a hole in the roof, perhaps he shouted, "You're crazy!" or lay there quietly, in awe of their creative persistence. And as they lowered him down through the roof to the feet of Jesus, he must have felt excited or perhaps a bit self-conscious. Imagine all eyes on you.

When his mat touched the ground and he looked up and saw Jesus standing there and gazed into His eyes, did he feel peace and calm like he'd never felt before? Jesus told him, "Get up, take your mat and walk" (v. 9). When he did, his friends must have been cheering uncontrollably.

I've often wondered what would have happened if the paralytic had refused to receive help from his friends.

His life reminds me that surrendering my pride so that I can receive from others is a necessary part of my grief journey. I've learned to accept encouraging words, cards, gifts, prayers, hugs, meals, advice, financial support, and practical help. At times I've felt self-conscious and wanted to resist receiving. That's when God reminds me of a paralyzed man fortunate enough to have compassionate friends who helped him hope again so he could stand up. Although Scripture doesn't tell us what happened after the paralytic was healed, I'd like to believe he comforted others with the comfort he had received with gusto.

Are you in need of a lift? What's keeping you from receiving help? Do you need people to support you? Why not ask God to provide them? Who in your life has lifted you up through your grief journey? Take a moment right now to thank God for each of them.

God, I can feel so paralyzed by my grief. When others try to help me, I push them away. Please help me to surrender my pride to You and allow others to encourage me. Be the Healer of my attitude and replace my resistance with a willingness to receive assistance. Thank You for the caring people in my life. Lord, use them to lift my soul so that someday I will be able to give again. Amen.

My Journey

_____

_____

_____

_____

_____

_____

_____

_____

_____

_____

_____

_____

Part 7: Accepting

Your Journey
Through Accepting

Accepting: *to receive with consent, to give admittance or approval to, to endure without protest, to receive as true, to understand*

God grant me the serenity to accept the things I cannot change; courage to change the things I can; and wisdom to know the difference.
—Reinhold Niebuhr

Devotion 27

SEATED AT THE
TABLE OF ACCEPTANCE

*"The kingdom of heaven is like a king who prepared a
wedding banquet for his son. He sent his servants to those
who had been invited to the banquet to tell them to come, but
they refused to come. . . . So the servants went out into the
streets and gathered all the people they could find, the bad as
well as the good, and the wedding hall was filled with guests."*

—MATTHEW 22:2–3, 10

*Y*our table is ready."

I love to hear those words. They assure me
that my hungry stomach will soon be satisfied. Most of
the time I don't mind waiting—unless, of course, I see
others who arrived after me seated first. It just doesn't
seem fair.

Though most of us don't long for death the way we long to be seated at a table in a restaurant, it is true that God is preparing a table for us in heaven. But sometimes others are called there before we are. It may be a child just beginning life's journey, a spouse we think we can't live without, or a friend in the prime of her life passionately serving Jesus. We may not understand why. It doesn't seem fair. Did God make a mistake? We question, doubt, vent, or cry until nothing else is left to feel. That's usually when we give up and accept the inevitable. In spite of unanswered questions, accepting the death of your loved one is possible.

Your journey to accepting your loved one's death can be as simple as saying, "I give up trying to understand" or "God, I surrender my loved one's death to You."

There is no right way to reach acceptance. Each grief journey is personal. But you will know when you have arrived. You may sense a peace or calm that you haven't felt in quite some time, as if a burden has been lifted so you can smile again. The relief you experience may remind you of how you feel when the hostess announces, "Your table is ready."

God sees the master list, and He understands the purpose and timing of everyone's death. Nothing we can do will change it. What we can do is accept it with His help.

I still struggle to accept the death of my son, cousin, friend, and many others. During times of doubt and despair, I picture the heavenly banquet table that's being adorned with white linen, fine china, crystal, and silver. I imagine an endless row of guests waiting to be seated and a divine Host calling each person by name. Perhaps as each person's name is called, they will be greeted by the Lord personally and led to a reserved seat. Imagine after all the guests have arrived and are seated, the Lord sits at the head of the table, and the banquet begins. I envision myself seated at the table of acceptance with my son, with Jesus Christ, and with other family and friends, including you! What a celebration that will be. I can hardly wait.

God, it seems as if I've waited so long for answers to my questions. Please help me surrender my uncertainty to You. Replace my despair with peace and my curiosity with calm. Thank You for being Jehovah-shalom, the Lord of peace. Thank You for being my heavenly Host and for preparing a royal banquet table for those who know You. Amen.

My Journey

_____

_____

_____

_____

_____

_____

_____

_____

_____

_____

_____

_____

_____

_____

_____

_____

_____

_____

_____

_____

_____

_____

_____

_____

_____

_____

LIGHTEN UP!

*Each of you should use whatever gift you have
received to serve others, as faithful stewards
of God's grace in its various forms.*

—1 PETER 4:10

K athe, lighten up and have some fun!" The counselor's directive startled me. My blank stare must have tipped her off that fun was a foreign concept for me during this season of grief. If she had suggested I work more or encourage others, I could have stepped out with enthusiasm to pursue those goals. But planning fun into my life wasn't my practice or priority. That was evident when she asked me to share what I enjoyed doing, and I struggled to name two things.

Then she instructed me to evaluate the fun people in my life. I listed everyone I interacted with and put a plus or a minus after each person's name to signify if that person energized me (+) or drained me (−).

I was surprised to discover that the majority of people in my life during that season were drainers. They consistently zapped me of energy with their hurtful comments, criticism, expectations, or negative attitudes. Although I valued each relationship, I had nothing left to give at that time.

My counselor asked me to do something extreme—to temporarily cross the drainers off my list and focus my time on the energizers. I resisted. What would the drainers think? Would they feel rejected or disown me? What would God think? Would this be a negative reflection on my faith?

My counselor persisted.

I realized that even Jesus had to take time to withdraw from the needy crowds to rejuvenate. He needed time for fun, laughter, and rest. Did Peter, James, and John fill that role for Him? When He needed a bed-and-breakfast getaway, did Mary, Martha, and Lazarus come to mind? When His cousin John was killed, He recognized that He needed time away to be silent, to grieve, and to be restored. Jesus kept His life in balance. He gave, but He allowed Himself to receive.

Giving has always come easier for me; it feels more spiritually correct than receiving. Yet the Bible tells us that there is a time for everything, and we are to allow others to build us up, accepting their acts of encouragement. My temporary withdrawal from certain people was a necessary step of obedience I needed to take.

But what about those I had to maintain daily contact with and couldn't retreat from? In those relationships, I set appropriate boundaries and told each person my counselor had directed me to focus on replenishing myself and to refuse to engage in negative or stressful conversations, situations, or activities for a time. She also encouraged me to be realistic with myself and honest with others about what they could expect from me. Most were understanding and sympathetic, and only a few expressed feelings of rejection and hurt.

That left the energizers on my list. Just the mention of the remaining names encouraged me. They were the type who loved me unconditionally, had no expectations, and made me feel refreshed and renewed. Focusing my attention on myself and allowing others to encourage me was uncomfortable at first and seemed a little self-indulgent, but I desperately needed replenishment. I let go of my pride and shared my need for fun and encouragement with them. God used them in a powerful way. Cards, calls, movies, shopping, praying together, a weekend away, and marshmallow fights were unexpected surprises. These special people helped me lighten up and have fun. They removed my fear of accepting love and attention from others and energized me so I could give again.

Planning fun into my grief journey is now a priority. I often enlist the help of others. When I need to laugh, I call a friend who tells jokes. When I need a day away, I call my friend who loves to be spontaneous and play. And I'm discovering all the fun things God has created for us to enjoy.

We will always have drainers and energizers in our lives, but when we allow ourselves to give and to receive, we can keep our lives in balance. It's good for me to let others know when I need encouragement and then to accept it with a smile!

What about you? Are you balancing your giving and receiving? Are you in need of encouragement from others? Do you need to take a break from the drainers and enlist more energizers? Ask God to show you how to lighten up and accept encouragement from others.

God, why is giving so much easier than receiving? Is my pride preventing me from accepting encouragement from others? I feel empty, with nothing to offer right now. I can't give like I used to, and that's hard for me. Help me discern which people are drainers and which are energizers. Give me courage to set boundaries for a time and to share my need to be encouraged. Help me joyfully accept laughter, fun, and acts of kindness from others. Recharge me with Your healing power, and turn my mourning into dancing so I can give again. Amen.

My Journey

_____

_____

_____

_____

_____

_____

_____

_____

_____

_____

Devotion 29

A TISSUE AND A CANDLE

Your word is a lamp for my feet, a light on my path.

—PSALM 119:105

arkness encircled Mary Magdalene's path as she set out for the tomb. I wonder if she recalled the events of the past few days in her mind as she walked. Was Jesus really dead? Perhaps she questioned if she were dreaming. Would she wake up and find Jesus walking beside her? Sorrow must have overwhelmed Mary as she stumbled on through the blackness. When she finally reached the tomb's entrance and saw the stone was moved, did she gasp in disbelief? Questions must have raced through her mind as she ran back to tell the disciples the tomb was empty. Later, when she returned and peered inside the tomb, did she quake with fear when she saw two angels and they asked, "Woman, why are you crying?" Perhaps their question validated her grief and forced her to pause and face her uncertainty.

"They have taken my Lord away, . . . and I don't know where they have put him," she replied (John 20:13). Then she turned around and saw Jesus standing there but didn't recognize Him. She thought He was the gardener until He spoke her name, "Mary." What indescribable joy she must have felt when Jesus' voice pierced her darkness and illuminated the truth. Her Teacher was alive. Maybe you're traveling a similar path to Mary's. Your loss feels like a dream, and darkness encircles you. You're stumbling through the blackness, yearning for the stone of disbelief to be rolled away. You want to face the truth, but how can you?

Accepting the truth of your loss and pressing on is a necessary part of your journey through grief. I've discovered that acceptance means more than just facing my loss; it also means facing the reality that painful emotions and darkness may be a part of my lifelong quest to deal with my grief. Accepting this new reality has increased my ability to cope.

When others ask how I've survived my loss, I simply reply, "With a tissue and a candle." I accept my emotions and know that I will need a tissue throughout my journey through grief. God is my Comforter and the One who wipes my tears.

I also accept the darkness that comes with grief and know that I will need a candle to light my path. God's Word is a consistent light to me. It's a lamp to my feet when I stumble through the darkness. It's the Lord's way of speaking to me. Like Mary, when I hear His familiar voice, I turn around. It pierces the darkness of my grief and illuminates my path with hope.

Are you resisting or accepting where you are? Do you need to face the truth that emotions and darkness may be a continuing part of your journey through grief? Maybe you're in need of a tissue and a candle to help you cope and press on in your journey to acceptance. God's Word will light your path. Turn to Him today.

God, I've been stumbling through the darkness of my grief, trying to face the truth. I want to move toward acceptance. I never realized that painful emotions and darkness could be part of my lifelong quest through grief. Help me accept that today and learn to cope. Comfort me, and be a lamp to my feet. When You call to me through Your Word today, help me turn to You. Remove the stone of my despair and replace it with life. Pierce my darkness and illuminate my path with the truth so I can press on. Amen.

My Journey

_____

_____

_____

_____

_____

_____

_____

_____

_____

_____

_____

_____

_____

_____

_____

_____

_____

_____

_____

_____

_____

_____

_____

_____

_____

_____

Devotion 30

"I'll Do It"

By faith Abraham, when called to go to a place . . . obeyed
and went, even though he did not know where he was going.
—Hebrews 11:8

When God calls you to do something for Him that doesn't fit your plans, how do you respond?

I heard a story about a manager who overheard an employee complaining that a task he had been assigned didn't suit him. In response to that complaint, the manager said, "You know, the world's a better place because Michelangelo didn't say, 'I don't do ceilings!'" That comment is worth reflecting on.

Would you agree that the world is a better place because:
Noah didn't say, "I don't do arks."
Moses didn't say, "I don't do mass migrations."
Mary didn't say, "I don't do virgin births."

Jesus didn't say, "I don't do crosses."

And the world will be a better place if you and I don't say, "I don't do _____."

We may miss opportunities to serve God in our journey through grief because we predetermine what we will and won't do without ever consulting Him. Disappointment, fear, denial, or a variety of other excuses can drive us to say, "I don't do grief."

At times I've even said, "I don't do grieving people." I didn't want to be surrounded by people who had lost loved ones, and I certainly didn't want to be labeled as a grief mentor. To my amazement, the more I resisted, the more God persisted. Unwanted opportunities flourished. Countless people who had lost a loved one contacted me needing encouragement. Complete strangers would stop me and begin to share about their losses. Several friends and family members encountered the loss of loved ones, so funerals and sympathy cards became part of my routine. Despite my whining, complaining, bargaining, and blatant refusals, God began to show me that He had a plan for my grief, and I needed to accept it. I finally broke down and told God, "I'll do it."

Little did I know that accepting my loss and the opportunity to be an encourager to those who grieve would change my life. Although grief is sometimes still a difficult journey for me, I'm thankful for God's patience as He guides me through the process. He continues to teach me the necessity of accepting His direction and calling in my life. If He hadn't transformed my *I don't do* thinking into *I'll do it* thinking, you wouldn't be reading this book.

What is God calling you to do in your journey through grief that you've been telling Him, "I don't do"? What steps do you need to take to accept your loss, as well as God's plan for using it? I encourage you to make the world a better place by telling God, "I'll do it!"

> God, You've been trying to help me accept my loss and use it to help others, but I've resisted. I've tried denying Your calling, hoping it would go away. I've tried bargaining with You. I've even tried running from You, but You always know just where to find me. The more I resist, the more You persist. I surrender! I want to do whatever You ask. Thank You for seeing my potential and for accepting me where I am. And thank You for giving me hope by saying "I'll do it" when You sent Your Son to die for me on the cross. Amen.

My Journey

_____

_____

_____

_____

_____

_____

_____

_____

_____

_____

_____

_____

_____

_____

_____

_____

_____

_____

_____

_____

_____

_____

_____

_____

Part 8: Praising

Your Journey
Through Praising

Praising: *to commend, glorify, worship, value*

*Our griefs cannot mar the melody of our praise; they
are simply the bass notes of our life song, "He hath
done great things for us, where of we are glad."*
—C. H. Spurgeon

*Praise flourishes as you weed and water and fertilize your
spiritual garden in which it grows. It becomes more constant
as you nurture your soul on God's Word and walk in His
ways, depending upon the Holy Spirit. It gets richer and
more spontaneous as you grow in your knowledge of how
worthy the Lord is to receive honor and glory and praise.*
—Ruth Myers, *31 Days of Praise*

Devotion 31

THE PATHWAY THROUGH PAIN

> *David noticed that his attendants were whispering*
> *among themselves, and he realized the child was dead.*
> *"Is the child dead?" he asked. "Yes," they replied, "he*
> *is dead." Then David got up from the ground. After he*
> *had washed, put on lotions and changed his clothes, he*
> *went into the house of the Lord and worshiped.*
>
> —2 SAMUEL 12:19–20

The empty chair, the barren bed, the unworn clothes in the closet, and the silence—all these remind us that we will never again see our loved one on earth. Our pain feels fresh and sharp again.

King David understood the anguish of grief. Every time he walked by his son's room he must have sensed death's presence. What would life be like without his child? No more laughter. No tucking him in at night. No birthdays, no heir to his throne.

David had pleaded for God to spare his child. But his son had died. Then David's pain drove him to God. He knew he needed to be in God's presence after his son's death. Remarkably, David recognized that the pathway through pain was praise.

Praise focuses on who God is and on His nature, character, and power. Like David, when we think of who God is or of something He has done, our hearts overflow with gratefulness. It's all right if our praise emerges in the midst of our pain. Joyful praise isn't necessarily more valuable to God. He doesn't enjoy our praise on the basis of how warm and happy we feel, but rather on the condition of our hearts.

As C. S. Lewis has said, we may honor God more in our low times than in our peak times. When we find ourselves depressed or wiped out emotionally and yet praise Him anyway, we may bring Him special joy. We may look around at a world from which God seems to have vanished and still choose to trust Him and praise Him in spite of how we feel.

Praise brings the refreshment of God's presence into our situation. It helps us view our loss through different lenses by focusing on God rather than our circumstances. Often this change of vision transforms the atmosphere around us. In turn, a new attitude causes people to react differently to us, and we begin to exert a creative and uplifting influence on others.

As we fill our lives with praise, God will reveal Himself to us in new ways. He'll also reveal Himself through us to others.

Who is God to you? What has He done for you? Praise Him!

God, I praise You for being my faithful Father. You're always there to hold me. You are my Comforter who wipes away my tears. I praise You for being my companion through the journey of grief. You are the Healer of my broken heart. When I focus my attention on You and not on my circumstances, my pain lessens. Help me continue to praise my way through the pathway of pain. Amen.

My Journey

_____

_____

_____

_____

_____

Devotion 32

MOUNTAIN MOVER

Lord, you have been our dwelling place throughout
all generations. Before the mountains were born
or you brought forth the whole world, from
everlasting to everlasting you are God.

—PSALM 90:1–2

Kathe, we've decided to give you a Labor of Love shower," my friends announced.

I was stunned. I thought, *Most women would be thrilled to be showered with baby gifts, but when your baby is expected to die, a shower is just one more painful reminder of your loss.*

"We know your situation is unique, but you deserve to be encouraged," my friends explained. "We'd like to give you an uplifting day of singing, prayer, food, and surprises."

I was touched. Even though the shower seemed a bit

odd, I sensed God smiling at the whole idea. I began to look forward to my Labor of Love shower and to the support and encouragement I would receive, even if it came in an unconventional way.

The day of the shower, when I entered the family room, I was amazed to see nearly fifty women amid the streamers and balloons. A "Labor of Love" banner filled with personalized notes adorned the wall. The outpouring of love and encouragement was overwhelming.

My friend Ginger touched my arm. "It's really hard for me to be here today," she tearfully admitted. "I almost didn't come."

I gave her a reassuring hug and thanked her for attending. As if on cue to break the tension, a woman handed us song sheets and directed us to our seats as a symphony of singing voices filled the room.

As the last chorus was sung, I waddled to the center of the room and plopped down in a designated chair. Caring eyes flooded my vision. I suspected many women had hidden questions. How was I coping with the impending loss of my baby? Did I feel angry or afraid? What was God teaching me through this experience? Did I believe God would perform a miracle?

During the past several months, I had lived with the

painful prognosis that death was imminent for my baby. Yet I clung to the hope that God would perform a physical miracle. My conviction led me on a lonely journey that left me feeling misunderstood by others. Most believed I was in denial and unable to face reality; I was convinced that my stand of faith was how God wanted me to respond. I endured silent ridicule, questioning stares, and thoughtless comments. At times I chose to isolate myself from others so I wouldn't be tempted to waver in my belief that God would heal my child.

God, please give me the right words to say, I prayed as I sat surrounded by women waiting for me to speak.

Over the next few moments, I recalled the bittersweet journey of my surprise pregnancy after fifteen years of marriage, infertility, and adoption. I shared how I enjoyed carrying my unborn child and believed that God was able to heal our baby, but that even if He chose not to, I would still trust Him. The words that I blurted out next surprised me. "We all face mountains in our life journey. They block our view, they paralyze us with fear and hopelessness, they stand as a monument of what we can't control. But the pathway to faith and victory is to focus on the Mountain Mover and not on the mountain."

Tears stung my eyes as I pondered my own words

and remembered the many personal mountains God had moved for my roomful of friends.

At that point, Ginger left the room. Moments later I saw her maneuvering through the crowd toward me. She smiled and handed me a soft, gray bundle. "Kathe, I had to give you this after I heard you speak. It's been in the trunk of my car for several months. Now I know why I never took it out."

I looked at the ordinary gray T-shirt. Slowly I unrolled it. When I saw its inscription, I gasped. "Mountain Movers . . . faith that moves mountains. Matthew 17:20," it read.

God affirmed me in a powerful, visual way that day. "Mountain Movers" became my labor-and-delivery motto. I even ordered T-shirts so my friends could sport the Mountain Movers motto when they came to the hospital during my delivery. But God surprised us all when a man in the waiting room asked my friends whether they knew Ginger. He explained that he had created the Mountain Mover T-shirts for her. I could almost hear God chuckling and saying, *If I can orchestrate it so the man who created your T-shirt is at the hospital during your delivery, don't you think that I, the Creator of the universe, the almighty Mountain Mover, am surely with you?*

My long night of labor was difficult, but I kept focusing

on the T-shirt hanging on my hospital wall. God was faithful to the motto He had given me. He moved my mountain of fear and replaced it with faith. He used my situation to soften hospital workers' hearts, moving them closer to Himself. He moved multitudes across the country to pray for us. And even though my son didn't survive, God gave me the privilege of being his mother and the comfort of knowing I will see him again in heaven.

What about you? What mountain are you facing today that blocks your view? I encourage you to focus not on your mountain of grief, but on the only One strong enough to move it. Then praise Him for His faithfulness.

God, I praise You for being bigger than the mountain I'm facing today. I'm sorry that I've allowed it to obstruct my view of You. Help me trust You. Help me believe You. Replace my fear with faith. Please help me fix my eyes on Your almighty power and faithfulness today. Remind me of the many mountains that You have already moved in my life. Thank You for being my Mountain Mover today. Amen.

My Journey

Devotion 33

PAIN-PRODUCING PRAISE

*Praise be to the name of God for ever and ever; wisdom and
power are his. He changes times and seasons; he deposes
kings and raises up others. He gives wisdom to the wise and
knowledge to the discerning. He reveals deep and hidden
things; he knows what lies in darkness, and light dwells
with him. I thank and praise you, God of my ancestors.*

—DANIEL 2:20–23

*P*ain often produces something of great value. I'm
reminded of that every time I see a pearl. Oddly, the
priceless pearl began as a pebble or particle of sand within
an oyster's shell. This painful irritant prompted the oyster to secrete a calcium-like substance that hardened into
smooth, concentric circles around the object. When the
oysters are harvested and their shells are pried open, often
you'll discover a valuable gem—the product of their pain.

That's how I feel about losing a loved one. Our pain can often produce something of great value. During my own grief journey, the book *31 Days of Praise* by Ruth Myers became a priceless gem to me. It pointed me to a new understanding of praising God in the midst of my pain.

I had always believed that praising was synonymous with smiles, happiness, and enthusiasm, not something that could encompass tears and pain. Now I realize that praising allows us to rely on God and focus on His character and attributes in spite of our pain.

Ironically, the gem of a book that soothed my soul began after a young wife sojourned in Taiwan, the Philippines, and Hong Kong during her first husband's intense bout with cancer before the Lord called him home. During her years as a widow with two young children, her book was born. It flowed out of truths that had long motivated her to trust and worship the Lord in the varied seasons and experiences of life. I'm grateful to Ruth Myers for allowing God to transform her painful irritant of loss into a product of great value that has touched my life and that of many others as well.

When you reflect on your loss and the pain it inflicts, remember that pain can prompt you to call out to God in praise. Praise isn't denying the pain; it's pronouncing who

God is in the midst of your pain. Praise is a priceless gem that you can discover today. Allow your pain to produce praise.

Almighty God, Author of life and death, You are compassionate and understanding. You accept me today where I am and love me. You are my Hope-Giver, my Encourager, my Friend. Praising You doesn't come easily for me because my life is so painful. Use my pain to prompt me to praise You. Transform my irritant of loss into the priceless gem of knowing You in a deeper way. Amen.

My Journey

_____

_____

_____

_____

_____

_____

_____

_____

_____

_____

Devotion 34

DEEP ROOTS

"But blessed is the one who trusts in the LORD, whose confidence is in him. They will be like a tree planted by the water that sends out its roots by the stream. It does not fear when heat comes; its leaves are always green. It has no worries in a year of drought and never fails to bear fruit."

—JEREMIAH 17:7–8

A storm ravaged my neighborhood. Broken tree limbs cluttered the streets, and uprooted tree trunks blanketed the lawns. But some trees stood unharmed by the ferocious wind. How had they survived the storm?

I realized that a tree's strength is hidden beneath the surface, in its roots. The deeper the roots, the stronger the tree. The trees with deep roots were anchored securely and endured the storm, unlike their shallow-rooted friends.

When the storms of grief rage through my life, am I

ripped apart, or do I persevere? What keeps me anchored and standing tall?

As I took inventory of my varied responses during my grief journey, I realized that my strength came from being rooted in God's presence. When I focus on who God is, I am able to stand. When I choose to see God as the light in the midst of my darkness, or my rock in the midst of my crumbling emotions, or my shield when I feel as if I'm being hit with arrows of doubt and discouragement, I can cope with grief. But when I take my eyes off Him and focus on myself or my situation, I feel uprooted.

I've decided to stay rooted in praising God. When the winds of loneliness try to blow me over, I see God as my companion. When the hail of despair pounds at my door, I welcome God in as my hope. If the freezing rain of fear begins to creep into my soul, I cry out to God as my warm encourager. Whatever I sense is my greatest need at the time, one of God's characteristics counterbalances it.

Whether we choose to acknowledge Him or not, He is our root of security. It's up to us how we choose to respond.

Jeremiah encouraged us to grow deep spiritual roots and respond to our circumstances by trusting God. By the world's standards, Jeremiah was a failure. For forty years he served as God's spokesman, but nobody listened. He was rejected, ignored, mistreated, and alone much of his life. Yet he survived by looking beyond his circumstances with faith and courage to God.

When we choose to be rooted in God's presence and to focus on Him, we can be assured that, no matter what takes place, we can rely on His wisdom, goodness, mercy, and truth. Like Jeremiah, we can have deep spiritual roots that will enable us to endure the storms of grief.

What storms are you facing? Do you feel ripped apart and broken, or are you standing tall? You can weather any circumstance by being rooted in God's presence.

God, thank You for being with me through my storms of grief. You've been my Comforter when I cried, my Strength when I was weak, my Sight when I couldn't see past my circumstances, my Light in the dark night of my soul. Forgive me for the times I didn't acknowledge Your presence. I know You never left me. Reveal Yourself to me in every situation I face, and help me stay rooted in You. Amen.

My Journey

_____

_____

_____

_____

_____

_____

_____

_____

_____

_____

_____

_____

_____

_____

_____

_____

_____

_____

_____

_____

_____

_____

_____

_____

_____

_____

Devotion 35

JOURNEY TO THE
SCHOOLHOUSE OF PRAISE

Praise the LORD, my soul; all my inmost
being, praise his holy name.

—PSALM 103:1

*D*own a dusty, gravel road in the middle of nowhere stands a little country schoolhouse nestled between a grove of pine trees and a church cemetery with a white picket fence. A woman clad in a dark, floor-length dress emerges from the schoolhouse and clangs a bell. Children scurry up the rickety wooden steps and file one by one through the doorway to take their familiar seats. The room is divided into two sections: larger desks on one side for the older children and smaller desks on the other for the younger ones.

In the back corner stands a makeshift sink: an orange crate turned on its end with a wash pan filled with water atop it. In the other corner is the coatrack and a shelf filled with lunch pails. The aroma of books and wood fills the air along with a hint of smoke from the wood-burning stove. As is her habit, the teacher shares Scripture and prayer and then walks behind her desk to the front wall.

All eyes peer at her hand as she picks up the chalk and begins to print on the blackboard: A . . . B . . . C . . . She continues until Z and then turns to face the class. "Today's lesson will be to focus on words that start with each letter of the alphabet," she announces.

One by one the children take turns walking to the blackboard to scribble a word for their assigned letter. Words like *apple*, *butterfly*, *cat*, *dog*, *frog*, and *snake* adorn the blackboard.

The teacher nods and continues, "Class, now I want you to take out a sheet of paper and write down your own personal words for each letter. Think about things you enjoy, things that are special to you."

The teacher collects the papers and begins to review them at her desk. She is amazed to discover the variety of words the students have written to express what each letter means to them personally. A—art, A—acorn-picking,

A—August, A–automobiles, A—azaleas, A—Ann. She realizes an important truth: though the letters are the same, what they represent for each person is different.

Praising our way through grieving is much like this one-room schoolhouse scene. We have our grief in common, yet may be at different stages of our learning. But the one constant we can count on is God. As we write the ABCs of who God is on the blackboard of our souls, the words we each choose to describe Him are personal. Go ahead and try it. Write a word for each letter to describe who God is to you. And when you've finished, tell Him. He will love to receive your ABCs of praise.

God, I acknowledge You as my Teacher. Sometimes I feel like a slow learner when it comes to praising You through my pain. I understand that grief is a required course for me, and I'm in the process of learning more about it. Praise is another. I know I'm not alone in this schoolhouse of learning. You stand at the front of the classroom and point me to the spiritual blackboard. *Who am I to you?* You ask. *Tell Me today.*

I will, Lord. You are . . .

A_____   N_____

B_____   O_____

C_____   P_____

D_____   Q_____

E_____   R_____

F_____   S_____

G_____   T_____

H_____   U_____

I_____   V_____

J_____   W_____

K_____   X_____

L_____   Y_____

M_____   Z_____

Amen.

My Journey

Part 9: Being

YOUR JOURNEY THROUGH BEING

Being: *the quality or state of having existence, life, essence, personality, presence, reality, actuality; to endure; to dwell*

If the pace and the push, the noise and the crowds are getting to you, it's time to stop the nonsense and find a place of solace to refresh your spirit.
—CHARLES R. SWINDOLL, *Intimacy with the Almighty*

"Be still, and know that I am God."
—PSALM 46:10

BEING WITH THE SHEPHERD

*The LORD is my shepherd, I lack nothing. He makes
me lie down in green pastures, he leads me beside quiet
waters, he refreshes my soul. He guides me along the
right paths for his name's sake. Even though I walk
through the darkest valley, I will fear no evil, for you are
with me; your rod and your staff, they comfort me.*

—PSALM 23:1–4

The funeral was over, the crowd was gone, and the
tension of the past few days had diminished. I had
no more tears to cry. Exhausted, I felt hollow and alone.
How do I begin to heal? How do I get back to normal?

Silence penetrated our home. Usually I would have
welcomed it, but instead of soothing me, it made me feel
awkward. I was relieved when the doorbell rang.

A stranger stood at my door carrying a tray of food.

She smiled and explained that she had prepared a meal for our family. When I invited her in, she brushed by me, headed for the kitchen, and began to unpack.

"Enjoy your dinner," she said and turned to leave. "You can expect others to bring meals for the next two weeks."

I was touched that so many people would volunteer to cook dinner for us. How humbling to think that in such a busy, demanding world, others had found time to be used by God to provide for me.

Over the next couple of weeks, I began to experience "being" in a new way. I used to equate being with silence and rest, but I began to realize that the state of being encompassed much more. Being is the very essence of who we are: being in need, being available, being servants, and being served. I realized that being weak, being tired, and being in need were okay. Those conditions allowed God to use others as providers.

Little did I know that being served by others for the next couple of weeks would also give me another unexpected gift: time to focus on being with God. Instead of cooking, I used my time to pray, journal, read the Bible, and listen to God. During that time, God allowed me to relate to Him as my Shepherd, and He encouraged me through Psalm 23. I realized that God had provided a season of being for me to rest, to be restored, and to be provided for. He took care of daily needs, enabling me to be physically and spiritually nourished. And He showed me the importance of being with Him during my journey through grief.

Being with the Shepherd now forms a necessary part of every day. Some days I set my dining room table for two and invite God to be with me for breakfast as I read His Word. Other days I schedule time with Him in my backyard, at the bagel shop, or behind closed doors at my office to sit in silence and just listen.

A few times throughout the year I schedule a DAWG Day (Day Alone with God). Whether I check into my friend Brenda's guestroom, take a drive out of town, go to a park, or spend a day at the cemetery, I spend time with God and allow Him to be the Shepherd who restores me. In turn, I ask Him to reveal ways I can be available to others to pass on the gift of "being" with Him.

Never underestimate the eternal value of preparing a meal for someone. Just as I did, others might find they've been given the unexpected gift of time to be with the Shepherd. That, after all, is the greatest gift a grieving person can receive.

God, You are my Shepherd, the Provider, and the Restorer of my soul. Thank You for prompting people to be available and to serve. Thank You for the times when I'm in need and for meeting those needs in unexpected ways. Thank You for being with me in my journey through grief. Help me make being with You a priority—a necessary appointment that I look forward to. Restore me during those times, and show me ways I can encourage others to be with You. Amen.

My Journey

_____

_____

_____

_____

_____

_____

_____

_____

_____

_____

BEING IN THE DARKNESS

You, LORD, keep my lamp burning; my
God turns my darkness into light.
—PSALM 18:28

W hen I was a child, I used to dread walking into my bedroom after dark. I would stand at my doorway and peer into the unlit room, which seemed eerie and uninviting. My imagination ran wild with thoughts of what might lurk in my closet or beneath my bed. Frequently I bargained with my parents and made excuses to postpone bedtime. Eventually I had no choice but to face my fear and enter the darkness.

Loss leads to darkness. Darkness comes no matter how hard we try to avoid it. However threatening the dark might appear, eventually we must face it and enter it alone.

Darkness descended on me several months after my son's

death. For the first few weeks, I was inundated with phone calls, letters, and visitors. I quickly returned to work and filled my calendar with activity. People and organizations sought me out and asked me to share about my loss. In addition to my work, speaking, and being a wife and mother, I assumed additional community leadership roles. I didn't realize that darkness loomed ahead and that all my activity was only postponing it.

When I discovered I was pregnant again, I was thrilled. I believed God was healing my hurt. But then I miscarried our baby. I was devastated and couldn't believe I was facing another loss so soon.

I woke up one morning and didn't want to get out of bed. I felt myself slipping into a dark cave of despair and dread, with no motivation or desire to be around people. When others spoke to me, I had difficulty hearing what they were saying. Never had I experienced such emptiness, anguish, and aloneness. Would I live in darkness forever?

A few days later, I read that the quickest way to reach the light of day isn't to run west toward the setting sun, which seems natural, but to do the opposite. Head east and enter the darkness until you come to the sunrise. At that moment I knew that my darkness was unavoidable. I could try to outrun it or postpone it, but eventually I would have to walk into the darkness of my loss to be transformed.

I made a decision to journey into darkness, to yield to my pain and loss. When I gave myself permission to grieve wherever or whenever, intentionally or spontaneously, I was surprised by how free I felt and how inoffensive my decision was to others. It actually encouraged others to mourn their losses as well.

I scheduled time for solitude so I could be in the darkness alone. Sometimes I slipped away to my bedroom and listened to music, mostly instrumentals or praise and worship; sometimes I took a bath and read a book; at other times I went for a drive. Mostly I curled up on my couch late at night and stared into the darkness, reliving my loss and what could have been.

Praying was hard for me. Sometimes all I could do was groan or mumble a few words to tell the Holy Spirit to pray on my behalf. This gave God an opportunity to draw near to me.

The regular ritual of being in the darkness was painful but productive. It became sacred to me, and my spirit yearned for this authentic time of grieving. Being in the darkness enlarged my soul. I didn't get over my loss, but I learned to live with it. I sensed God's comfort. The light of His love illuminated the dark places in my heart, and both darkness and light helped to transform me.

Darkness is a continuous part of my journey through

grief. It is not a one-time experience, but rather it is a constant companion to me as I discover new dimensions of my loss. Unlike it was in my childhood, being in the dark isn't something I dread or fear now, but a place I willingly enter into, a place where God can draw near and change me.

What about you? Are you afraid of the dark? Have you been running from it and postponing your entry into it? Or have you plunged into the night-depths of your soul to be transformed by the experience?

You can't escape the dark, so stop trying. Go ahead, enter the darkness. And remember, you won't be alone. God is your Comforter, Intercessor, and Light. His love will see you through and enlarge your soul.

God, darkness is closing in on me. I've been trying to avoid the inevitable, and I need You to help me realize that being in the darkness is part of my journey through grief. I don't want to dread or fear it, but I want to embrace it and allow You to use it to change me. Slow me down, Lord, and allow me to face my pain and loss. Be my Comforter, Encourager, Companion, and Light. Illuminate the dark night. Show me today how being in the darkness has enlarged and will enlarge my soul. Amen.

My Journey

_____
_____
_____
_____
_____
_____
_____
_____
_____
_____
_____
_____
_____
_____
_____
_____
_____
_____
_____
_____
_____
_____
_____
_____
_____
_____
_____

SLOW DOWN AND DETOUR
TO THE SCHOOL OF BEING

*"Come to me, all you who are weary and
burdened, and I will give you rest."*
—MATTHEW 11:28

As Rich handed me an envelope, I could tell by my husband's anxious look that something important was inside. Curiosity and excitement gripped me. *Maybe it's an unexpected check or a letter announcing I've won a contest*, I thought. I ripped open the envelope to claim my treasure, only to find an official-looking document with my picture on it.

To my disappointment and surprise, I discovered that my "treasure" was a photo radar traffic ticket. I had been caught speeding. *It must be a mistake*, I thought. However, the snapshot of a woman behind the wheel driving my vehicle with my license plate proved I was guilty. My violation read, "Speed greater than reasonable and prudent."

I considered my options: pay the fine, contest the citation by appearing in court, or attend a defensive driving school. My husband and I agreed I should go to school.

"My life is so hectic. How can I fit two nights of class into my schedule?" I whined.

Rich gazed deep into my eyes. "Maybe it's time you slowed down, Kath."

His words hit a nerve. *Maybe he's right*, I thought. *Why do I have this compelling need to jam my schedule with activity?* As I pondered this question, I realized that since my son's death, work and busyness had been my constant companions. In some strange way, they comforted me. I equated activity with productivity. Yet as I examined my lifestyle, I could see that I was in the speed trap of grief—going too fast to feel the pain of my loss. The speed of my activity was greater than reasonable and prudent, and I needed to slow down.

That scared me. I liked the fast pace, and slowing down would force me to focus on the road signs of my loss. The idea felt uncomfortable and inconvenient—like a road under construction, filled with bumps, holes, and dirt.

Martha must have understood this all too well; she struggled with lessening her load of activity. She loved multitasking and could accomplish more in one day than most people she knew. She thrived on noise and "doing," unlike her sister, Mary, who could ignore her work and spend hours reading, reflecting, or listening to a friend.

What a waste of productive time, Martha must have thought as she glared at her sister, who was sitting content-edly at their guest's feet. Perhaps her anger and resentment flared. *I'm doing all the work, and she's doing nothing! It's time Mary picked up the pace and got busy!*

Did she storm into the room expecting Jesus to agree with her and respond to her demand to instruct her sister to help her? Instead, to Martha's surprise, He gazed into her eyes and gently replied, "Martha, Martha . . . you are worried and upset about many things, but few things are needed—indeed only one. Mary has chosen what is better, and it will not be taken away from her" (Luke 10:41–42).

Jesus' words must have hit a nerve in Martha. *Maybe He's right*, she may have thought. *Why do I have this com-pelling need to stay busy?* Perhaps Martha pondered this question, realizing she felt uneasy when she slowed down. It forced her to be alone with herself, with her thoughts, with her questions and fears, and with God. Maybe that scared her. Yet when she looked at Mary, did her soul yearn to slow down and readjust her pace and her priorities? Did she long to "be" instead of "do"?

Filling your life with too much activity can prevent growth and healing in your journey through grief. Sooner or later you will get caught in the speed trap of grief, forced to realize that you are driving yourself at a speed that is neither reasonable nor prudent. It's time to slow down! You can't pay off this offense with money, and the longer you contest it, the longer you put off your restoration.

Clearly the best solution is to become a student in the school of being. It may be hard for you to readjust your pace and your priorities. You may feel uncomfortable being alone with yourself, with your thoughts, with your questions and fears, and with God. Like Martha, you need to slow down and take the detour to the school of being. It's a necessary part of your journey.

God, my life is hectic; I'm speeding out of control. Busyness and work have been my companions since my loss. Activity comforts me and distracts me. I'm afraid to slow down and be alone with myself and with You.

I've been filling the void with activity. Please forgive me. I want to readjust my pace and my priorities to allow You to help me grow and heal. Be like a radar to my soul and slow me down, Lord. Help me take this detour and become a student in the school of being. Amen.

My Journey

_____

_____

_____

_____

_____

_____

_____

_____

_____

_____

_____

_____

_____

Devotion 39

JOURNEY TO THE COCOON OF BEING

Then I prayed to Jehovah. "Lord," I pled, "you are my
only place of refuge. Only you can keep me safe."

—PSALM 142:5 TLB

*T*he process of adapting to loss and change takes energy. Grief can be draining, causing us to feel more tired and irritable than usual. In turn, our ability to focus and function in other areas of our lives may be lessened. And we may want to isolate ourselves from others, to hide in the safety of our homes.

When we're going through grief, we need to be gentle with ourselves. We don't have to measure up to who we normally are and what we usually can deliver. Giving ourselves permission to lighten our load, to do less and to just *be*, is healthy and essential. We're changing. Our physical and emotional needs may be different now, requiring us to welcome more rest, quiet, and comfort from others. We may be more needy. We may find it necessary to remove ourselves from activity for a season and enter a time of solitude. Our grief journey may lead us to a place where we need to cocoon ourselves so we can be transformed.

God reminded me of this when I noticed a caterpillar, who was ugly, vulnerable, and welcome prey to any bird in the neighborhood. *How will it survive?* I wondered. Then I realized that a caterpillar instinctively forms a silklike envelope around itself during a specific time in its journey. It ceases crawling on leaves and enters a state of just "being." The cocoon is the caterpillar's new home. It protects it from predators and the environment. It provides a safe place. During this season of being, the caterpillar undergoes change. Then one day it emerges from the cocoon, transformed into a butterfly. It has new energy and a different purpose. It has wings to fly. So it does.

Like the caterpillar, we may experience seasons in our journey through grief when we must just "be" to survive and to be transformed. We may have to relinquish expectations, activity, and responsibilities during this time. We may enter our cocoon feeling ugly, vulnerable, and prey to people's insensitivity and our own expectations. *How will*

I survive apart from others? we wonder. But we can. We are never alone, for God, our Transformer, is with us.

When we choose to leave our expectations and activity behind and enter the state of being, we undergo change. Rest and solitude comfort us. God speaks to us in our stillness, and we gain new insights about our loss. We learn the value of loving and caring for ourselves. We feel safe in God's arms and surrender to Him as He transforms the ugliness of our grief into something beautiful.

In time, we emerge from our cocoon of being, transformed into a new creature and excited about life again. We have new energy and an enlarged perspective about our loss. Before long, we take wing and fly!

God, I'm drained and exhausted from my loss. I feel as if I have nothing to give. It's hard to cope, and I don't know how to change. I know that I'm needy right now. Help me accept that about myself. Give me the strength to step away from expectations and activity for a season and cocoon myself so I can be renewed and restored. Wrap Your loving arms around me and change me. Transform the ugliness of my grief into something beautiful so that in time I can take wing and fly. Amen.

My Journey

_____

_____

_____

_____

_____

_____

_____

_____

_____

_____

_____

_____

_____

_____

_____

_____

_____

_____

_____

_____

_____

_____

_____

Devotion 40

ENJOY THE NOW

"Don't be anxious about tomorrow. God will take
care of your tomorrow too. Live one day at a time."
—MATTHEW 6:34 TLB

When my friend Lisa and I planned our annual getaway, we were expecting a stress-free, pampered weekend with no responsibilities, no schedules, and limitless conversation. But we soon discovered that our luxurious bed-and-breakfast was a dark, musty apartment cluttered with cobwebs and mismatched furniture. The "gourmet" breakfast that the brochure acclaimed was handed to us in a box when we checked in, and we were told to refrigerate it until morning.

My discontent and frustration ignited as I remembered our past getaways. Visualizing the multitude of better accommodations we had experienced and could be experiencing, I became more critical of the present situation. I longed for what had been and what could possibly be. I didn't want to be in this moment. I wanted out!

Fortunately, God is faithful to guide us back on the path of right thinking when we go astray. He used Lisa's gentle spirit, humor, and words to help me see that I was allowing the past to rob me of the present. Lisa chose to make the most of our experience, to seize the day and the moment. I, on the other hand, almost missed out on fun with a friend.

The time for doing and living is now. Too often in our journey through grief our todays slip by unnoticed because we are so preoccupied with tomorrow or absorbed with yesterday that we miss the here and now.

Our journey through grief may take us to an unexpected fork in the road with two road signs: What Was and What Will Be. Then we notice the third sign: What Is. At first we don't see it because we're so distracted by the other two. Which way do we allow our grief to take us? If we don't live in the now, we may be destroying our future. For it is the present that shapes the future.

I've learned to ask God, "Show me what's on Your agenda for me today, and help me make the most of the present." He may reveal a friend in need of encouragement, a verse to pray for my husband, or an inspiring idea for an article. Or God may remind me to simply embrace the present moment in silence, sensing His presence in the wind, the rain, or the sun.

God encourages us to enjoy the now. Like Lot's wife, who looked back to her past and was turned to salt, ignoring today and focusing on what life was like before our loved one died can have lasting consequences. We may miss out on moments that we will never be able to recapture: today's sunset, our child's hug, or a conversation with God. Although God does give goals and promises for the future, His focus is on the present. He is the God of the now.

What past regrets or future worries are robbing you of enjoying your present? Maybe it's time to release them to God and refocus your thinking on finding joy in the now.

God, I can see how the past and the future can distract me from enjoying the present. Please help me release my regrets and worries to You today. Forgive me for missing moments with others and with You. Help me enjoy being and living in the present and show me how to maximize my moments today. Amen.

My Journey

_____

_____

_____

_____

_____

_____

_____

_____

_____

_____

_____

_____

_____

_____

_____

_____

_____

_____

_____

_____

_____

_____

_____

_____

_____

Part 10: Celebrating

YOUR JOURNEY
THROUGH CELEBRATING

Celebrating: *to honor, memorialize, dedicate, keep; to demonstrate satisfaction by festivities or other deviation from routine; to hold up for public acclaim; to observe a holiday; to observe a notable occasion with festivities*

What the heart has once known, it shall never forget.
—AUTHOR UNKNOWN

Death is not a period bringing the sentence of life to a close
Like the spilling of a moment or the dissolution of an hour.
Death is a useful comma
Which punctuates, and labors to convince
Of more to follow.
—WILLIAM WALTER DEBOLT

Devotion 41

CELEBRATE YOUR
FRAMED MEMORIES

Always be joyful. Always keep on praying. No matter what
happens, always be thankful, for this is God's will for you
who belong to Christ Jesus. . . . But test everything that
is said to be sure it is true, and if it is, then accept it.
—1 THESSALONIANS 5:16–18, 21 TLB

Birthdays. Anniversaries. Special occasions. Holidays. They still come, but they are different now. Some who grieve choose to ignore them while others choose to celebrate them. Our response may change from year to year. Grief is a personal journey that allows each of us to celebrate our memories and to remember our loved ones in our own way and in our own time.

After my friend Margie lost her teenage son, Danny, in

an accident, she told me she dreaded holidays. In the past, holidays had been a time when her entire family gathered to celebrate, and Danny was usually the center of attention. Family pictures were a traditional part of their time together, and trying to come up with creative shots was part of their fun, always with the aim of outdoing the last family photograph. The family pictures displayed throughout Margie's home represented so many memories.

She chuckled as she recalled the year they dressed formally. "Danny must have been about three, and I had to buy him a suit just like the men. He looked so cute!" Margie's eyes misted with tears as she smiled. "I was in such a hurry to get everyone dressed that I forgot his underwear. I can still hear Danny's shrill little voice reminding me what I forgot."

Framed memories. Forever in our hearts. We may move the photos out of sight, but they are never out of mind.

Margie and her family decided to celebrate their personal memory of Danny with a family photograph Christmas card. They chose California sand, blue sky, and endless ocean as the backdrop because Danny loved the beach. Jagged rocks were used as the chairs. The family dressed casually, but what each person wore was special. Her husband and son-in-law wore Danny's favorite shoes. Her daughters wore jewelry Danny had given them. Another son-in-law sported Danny's favorite T-shirt. Margie's grandchildren tucked Danny's Legos in their pockets. And Margie held Danny's framed picture next to her heart.

Celebrating the memory of our loved ones is personal. Margie's family celebrated through a photograph. Your celebration may be different. You may choose visiting the cemetery, starting a scholarship fund in your loved one's name, or sharing your loved one's prized possessions with others.

Remembering our loved ones in special ways can be exhausting or exhilarating. When you look at your framed snapshots of memories, what do you see?

Let's remember . . . not to forget.

Gracious God, special events force me to face the memories of my loved one. I don't want to forget him (her), but sometimes it hurts to go through another special occasion without him (her). Help me remember the good. Use me to create something special as a memorial to my loved one's life. I want to frame his (her) memories and celebrate. Amen.

My Journey

Devotion 42

A TROPHY TO REMEMBER

*"Where, O death, is your victory? Where, O death,
is your sting?"... But thanks be to God! He gives
us the victory through our Lord Jesus Christ.*
—1 CORINTHIANS 15:55, 57

"On your mark. Get set. Go!" Racers thrust forward to capture the lead position. Partnering skill and technique with endurance, they press on to the finish line. The crowd cheers. How quickly the race ends, and then the victor steps forward, his face gleaming as an official awards him the championship trophy. That trophy stands as a monument of celebration, a symbol of his unyielding faith and perseverance to see his dream become reality.

Trophies are symbols of celebration and remembrance. When I see my son Jake's childhood trophies, I recall his first soccer season and his difficulty running in too-small shoes. His first swim team trophy reminds me of the summer when all his strokes looked the same. It also evokes a time just prior to his brother's death, a time when our family prepared to begin our grief journey.

Jake had prayed for a couple of years that God would give us a baby, and he was elated when his prayers were answered. When we learned our baby was expected to die from fatal birth defects, we realized the outcome could destroy our son's faith in God. How could we overcome this obstacle of grief? How could we transform death into something victorious?

Then we remembered how Jake loved trophies. *That's it!* we thought.

A few days later Jake walked into my hospital room to hold his baby brother and say good-bye to him. His face was solemn, and his eyes dimmed with disappointment as he touched his brother's fingers and toes. Jake knew he would never play catch with his little brother or kick a soccer ball to him.

"Jake, your brother has a gift for you."

I handed him a large trophy, decorated with a cross, a Bible, and praying hands.

Jake's eyes sparkled. "What does it say?" he asked as he pointed to the inscription.

With clarity and confidence I read, "To my big brother, Jake, because you prayed for me."

Celebrating and remembering our loved ones can bring healing to our souls. Whether the remembrance takes the form of a trophy, a recipe, a tradition, or a song, it doesn't matter. What matters is that we don't ignore our loved one's memory and the opportunity we have to celebrate him or her.

If you don't have remembrances of your loved one, create them. Start a celebration in his or her honor by giving an anonymous gift to a needy family on your loved one's birthday. Plant a tree or volunteer for a day at a homeless shelter. Celebrate your loved one with a sense of victory.

Lord, I've been running in the race of grief, trying to cross the finish line. At times I've stumbled, and it's been hard to get back up. But You've always been there. I want to press on and run with endurance and perseverance. Help me celebrate my loved one's memory. Show me how I can create opportunities to honor him (her) that will help others. Be my Victor and my Strength today, and help me remember and celebrate the victories You have given me in my race through grief. Amen.

My Journey

_____

_____

_____

_____

_____

_____

_____

_____

_____

_____

_____

_____

_____

_____

_____

_____

_____

_____

_____

_____

_____

_____

_____

_____

_____

_____

_____

Devotion 43

REMEMBER, YET CELEBRATE!

*Forgetting what is behind and straining toward what
is ahead, I press on toward the goal to win the prize for
which God has called me heavenward in Christ Jesus.*
—PHILIPPIANS 3:13–14

The aroma of fresh-cut flowers filled the air while candles flickered and radiated a warm, welcoming glow. People filed down the aisles as the organ played. Men clad in tuxedos and women in long gowns stood at the front of the room. The bridegroom stepped forward in eager anticipation. As his eyes scanned the pews, he saw elderly aunts, uncles, cousins, and a sister, but his eyes misted with tears as he stared at the empty places where his parents should have been seated. *I wish they were here to celebrate with me today,* he thought.

Childhood memories flooded his mind . . . being eight

years old and having two parents . . . then having only his mom. Then, at fifteen, his mom died too. He recalled passing his driver's test without them, moving away to college and enduring parents' weekends and the empty chairs at his high school and college graduations. Now his parents would miss his wedding day as well.

The bells chimed, announcing that his bride had arrived and his new life was about to begin. He turned from his past and looked to his future. In spite of the void in his life, he would celebrate this moment.

You may identify with this story, which is my husband's story. You, too, may have celebrated special occasions with a void in your life. You have wished your loved one was sitting around the table or in the pew, sharing milestone moments.

Does time heal the pain and fill the void? Sometimes.

Is celebrating still possible in your journey through grief? Absolutely! But it's a choice you must make.

I've often wondered how the disciples felt when they shared their first Lord's Supper without Jesus. Seeing His empty chair at the table must have felt strange. They would have to celebrate without Him. For a moment the mood may have been solemn as they felt the void of their Friend's companionship. They may have even reminisced about previous times with Jesus. When they passed the bread and the cup, did they recite Jesus' words, "Do this in remembrance of me" together (Luke 22:19)? Perhaps they realized the meaning of His words, that He wanted them to remember Him but press on. We reach a point in our journey through grief at which we have to integrate our past into our future and celebrate our new identity and direction. My husband continues to teach me the importance of celebrating as we encounter meaningful times in our family's life without his parents.

As we were on our way to the airport to leave for our honeymoon, Rich told me he had one surprise stop to make. My curiosity mounted as we drove through the gates of a wooded, estatelike setting. Rich took my hand and led me through a maze of stone markers. We stopped in front of a majestic pair, and he squeezed my hand and said, "I just wanted to remember them and include them in one of my happiest celebrations." Even though I never met Rich's parents, I know they were special. It's obvious every time I look at my husband.

It's okay to remember and to celebrate the joy of the moment.

God, I want to enjoy special occasions, but it's hard when I face an empty chair and realize my loved one can't share in my joy. My life has a void that others can't fill. Thank You for the memories I have of my loved one. Help me turn from my past and face the future. Be my Lord, who communes with me in my pain and in my joy. Help me journey on in my grief and celebrate. Amen.

My Journey

_____

_____

_____

_____

_____

_____

_____

_____

_____

_____

_____

_____

_____

Devotion 44

Journey from
Winter to Springtime

See! The winter is past; the rains are over and gone.
Flowers appear on the earth; the season of singing
has come, the cooing of doves is heard in our land.
—Song of Songs 2:11–12

Snowdrifts. Freezing temperatures. Howling winds. Frosted windowpanes. Gray skies. Icy driveways. Leafless trees.

Awaiting school closures was a Midwest winter ritual for me during my childhood. When fierce blizzards hit, I would be homebound for days. Being confined was frustrating and depressing at times. As more snow piled up against our house, I wondered how I was going to dig out from the drifts.

But over time the snow would melt, the temperatures

would climb, rays of sunshine would gleam, and stalks of green grass would poke through the ground. Springtime always ushered in new hopes, new life, and new looks. To shed layers of winter wool and sport a cheery new wardrobe was uplifting.

As we journey through grief, we may experience winter, when inner "frosting" occurs. We become resentful and frustrated by the storms of our circumstance. Blizzards of sadness blow through. We are snowed in, confined by our depression and hopeless of ever digging out.

When we feel this inner coldness, we need to remember how God renews the earth from the deadness of winter to springtime's vibrant beauty. His love melts the frost of our pain and grief.

Maybe today is the day to shed your winter wardrobe of grief and clothe yourself with a new spring look of hope and life. As you embrace the springtime, you may sense a new identity budding, possibilities blooming, and a renewed attitude poking up through the soil of your soul. Though you still miss your loved one, you feel alive again.

The winter of your grieving has passed, and you've survived it. It's time to celebrate springtime. Embrace it. Thank God. Live. Hope. Grow. Renew your mind and heart in the sunshine of God's love.

God, thank You for being with me through the winter of my grieving. As my Sunshine, defrost my frozen heart and attitude. Thank You that You will bring springtime to my soul with Your love. Renew my life, and clothe me with hope. Enable me to embrace the new opportunities and possibilities that You reveal to me today. Help me celebrate that winter will pass and embrace my journey to springtime. Amen.

My Journey

_____

_____

_____

_____

_____

_____

_____

_____

_____

_____

_____

_____

Part 11: Relating

YOUR JOURNEY
THROUGH RELATING

Relating: *to tell, to show, to establish a logical or casual connection between, to connect with*

Praise be to the God and Father of our Lord Jesus Christ, the Father of compassion and the God of all comfort, who comforts us in all our troubles, so that we can comfort those in any trouble with the comfort we ourselves receive from God.

—2 CORINTHIANS 1:3–4

Empathy is your pain in my heart.
—AUTHOR UNKNOWN

Devotion 45

LANDSCAPING LOSS INTO YOUR LIFE

Even the wilderness and desert will rejoice in those days;
the desert will blossom with flowers. Yes, there will be an
abundance of flowers and singing and joy! The deserts will
become as green as the Lebanon mountains, as lovely as
Mount Carmel's pastures and Sharon's meadows; for the
Lord will display his glory there, the excellency of our God.
—Isaiah 35:1–2 TLB

I went to see Carol the day after her husband died. When she came to the door, I greeted her with a box of tissues and a hug. Then I spent time listening to her recall her final hours with Bill. His sudden death had uprooted her sense of identity. Yesterday she was his business partner and wife. Today she was the business's sole owner and a widow. How could she relate to this new identity?

I knew nothing I could say would take away Carol's pain, but I wanted to give her words of hope. "Carol, you're in the process of landscaping."

She looked puzzled yet intrigued.

"Your loss is like a tree that's been chopped down in your backyard," I explained. Ironically, I had just read this illustration in the book *A Grace Disguised* by Jerry Sittser, and I was now relating it to Carol in my own words. "All that remains is a brown, ugly stump. That stump is a constant reminder of the beautiful tree you've lost. Each time you look out the window, all you can see is that stump. Eventually you will decide to do something about the stump. Instead of getting rid of it, you may decide to landscape around it. You might plant some shrubs, flowers, and other trees. In time, you may even decide to put a walkway leading up to it with a couple of benches to sit on. The stump will always remind you of the beautiful tree you lost, but someday it will be surrounded by a beautiful garden. Although your sorrow will remain, you'll have the opportunity to create a landscape around it so that what was once ugly will be part of a larger, lovely whole."

Carol nodded and squeezed my hand.

A few days later I received a call from Carol. "Kathe, you're never going to believe this. One of our large trees was too close to the house and needed to be cut down so I called a tree trimmer. When he arrived, I discovered he was also a pastor, and I told him about my loss and the stump story. He left but came back a few minutes later and said, 'Carol, the Lord told me to leave you a tree stump, so that's what I'm going to do.' I'm looking at my stump right now. I guess I'll need to start landscaping around it!"

Sooner or later we all suffer loss. It may come in little doses or big ones, suddenly or over time, privately or in a public setting. Loss is as much a part of everyday life as birth. Our experience of loss is not the defining moment that transforms us, but how we respond to that loss will largely determine the direction, the quality, and the impact of our lives.

Loss is a part of who I am. It's an integral part of my identity. I cringe when people ask me, "Are you over it yet?" You and I will never "get over" losing our children, our friends, or our loved ones. Instead, we must learn to integrate loss into our lives, to relate to it despite our feelings of uncertainty and inadequacy. Only God is able to guide us on this quest to learn simply to be who we are: widowed, childless, parentless, sisterless, friendless. Life can still be good, but just different than it was before.

Lord, part of my life has been cut down. My stump of loss reminds me of my loved one and who I once was but am no longer. Who am I now? Where do I go from here? Help me sort out who I am, reconsider my priorities, and determine new directions. You are the master Gardener. Transform my stump into a setting that is lush and beautiful. Show me how to relate to loss and to landscape it into my life in a way that glorifies You. Amen.

My Journey

_____

_____

_____

_____

_____

_____

_____

_____

_____

_____

_____

Devotion 46

GRIEF MENTOR

And the things you have heard me say in the
presence of many witnesses entrust to reliable people
who will also be qualified to teach others.

—2 TIMOTHY 2:2

Mentoring is as old as civilization. This natural, relational process allows the wiser, more experienced person to pass on insights to others. The Bible is rich with mentoring examples: Moses and Joshua, Paul and Timothy, Naomi and Ruth, and Elizabeth and Mary.

Webster's Dictionary defines *mentor* as a "trusted counselor or guide," but a mentor is much more. Mentors are like pathfinders who have scaled the mountain we intend to climb. They call down from higher up the mountain and encourage us to keep climbing. They warn us to watch the rocks, stay on the path, and not give up. They enlarge our perceptions and give us the confidence that, like them, we can overcome obstacles and achieve our dreams.

That's how God used Dottie in my life—to mentor me through my grief. Several years earlier she had lost a daughter with the same rare birth defect as my son. I had watched her endure the emotional pain of carrying a child destined to die and her grief journey through the years. Although we didn't communicate regularly, I always felt like a kindred spirit with her; and when I discovered I was to lose my child in the same way she had lost hers, I knew I could scale my mountain of grief because she had. Dottie was my mentor farther up the mountain, and her example gave me the courage to press on.

Being a grief mentor isn't a role I would have chosen, but God has enabled me to gain insights to share with others and to give them hope that God is the divine Connector who knows whom we need and when we need them. All we need to do is ask Him to connect us with those who can mentor us through grief—or whom we can mentor when we have journeyed farther down the path. Grief mentoring may consist of connecting with someone once, occasionally as needs arise, or regularly as a lifelong relationship.

Passing on what we know may require us to initiate the relationship. Many people long for encouragement in their grief journey but are afraid to voice their need. We may have to take the first step to offer encouragement. One way I've done this is to invite women who have lost a child on a chartered bus trip I sponsor each year for a day away for encouragement the week before Mother's Day. Although the women's ages, stages in life, and grief vary, they share a sisterhood of suffering. On the bus, we pass the microphone, and newcomers are encouraged to be real and share their feelings with no judgment. Veteran sojourners who have been transformed by their own experience with loss willingly offer themselves as the hands and feet of Jesus to comfort the newly grieving moms. Amazingly, God's power at work in and through their broken hearts spreads hope to others each year.

If others were to look to you as a grief mentor, what would you want them to see in you? What insights could you pass on that would give hope to others?

When I look back at each chapter of my life, I can name people God used as mentors. Most had "been there, done that." They shared their insights and knowledge with me. Some were there through timely cards, phone chats, texts, or online connections. Others invested long hours in person. Some were people I've never met but know from afar. God used people of all ages to give me hope and the courage to press on.

What about you? Who are the people who have influenced you through your grief journey, or whose lives you have influenced? Thank God, and thank them!

God, You are the divine Connector. You know exactly whom I need in my relational network to help me scale my mountain of grief. You also know who needs me to give them insight and encouragement. Thank You that I am not alone in my journey and that there are those who are willing to walk with me for a season. Show me who they are, and give me the courage to ask them to help me. Open my eyes to the needs of others, and use me to comfort them as well. Amen.

My Journey

_____

_____

_____

_____

_____

_____

_____

Devotion 47

CONNECTING THROUGH LOSS

No one has ever seen God; but if we love one another,
God lives in us and his love is made complete in us.

—1 JOHN 4:12

Reality hit when I saw the For Sale sign posted in the yard next door. Thirteen years of being neighbors with Theresa would soon come to an end. Through laughter and tears I recalled the life experiences we had shared: landscaping, garage sales, starting a home-based business, progressive dinner parties, coping with living far from family, becoming parents, new careers, divorce, and death.

God knew that Theresa was someone I needed during that season of my life. She understood how it felt to be childless and to endure Mother's Day with empty arms. When I labored through the adoption process, she was my cheerleader, ready to share her insights from adopting two children and being available to be our regular babysitter. It's hard to find neighbors like that.

In preparation for our new neighbors, we made a "neighbor wish list" and began to pray for our neighbors-to-be.

While waiting for God's answer, we experienced the fatal prognosis of our baby and our son's birth and death. Just weeks after his funeral, we saw a family walk out of the house next door. Could they be our new neighbors? We smiled and waved. They smiled and waved back. "Are you interested in the house?" we asked. They nodded and walked closer.

We told them that the best part about buying that house was to have us as neighbors! We all laughed. Then I noticed their two-year-old daughter and a small white bundle in the woman's arms. "How old is your baby?" I asked.

"Three months," she replied.

What a coincidence, I thought. *Our baby would be about that old.*

A few days later we saw the Sold sign. The young family we met would be our new neighbors. Stephanie was just the person I needed for that season of my life. She had experienced the death of an infant son a year earlier. The child's name was Jacob, our living son's name.

God knew exactly what He was doing by connecting

our lives. He gave me much more than I had prayed for. He hand selected a neighbor who understood my joy, my sorrow, and my journey through grief.

God, I'm beginning to realize that lots of people speak the language of loss; I'm not alone in my journey through grief. Others can relate to some of the challenges I face without my loved one. Thank You for being Jehovah-jireh, the God who provides, and for providing people to comfort me. In turn, use me to reach out to comfort others. Reveal to me a person I can encourage today. Amen.

My Journey

_____

_____

_____

_____

_____

_____

_____

_____

_____

JOURNEY TO THE POND OF RELATING

May the God of hope fill you with all joy and peace
as you trust in him, so that you may overflow
with hope by the power of the Holy Spirit.
—ROMANS 15:13

Whispering Pines. When Grannie and I saw the sign on the tree, we knew we had almost reached our destination. Just a few more steps through the woods, and then we saw it: the pond. The round body of brownish-green water in the middle of the forest was home to a multitude of creatures. A frog plopped into the water. A dragonfly landed on the floating lily pad. Tadpoles, turtles, and fish lived beneath the surface.

I picked up two rocks and clicked them together. I paused, then did it again. The frog replied and bellowed out a deep, *Croak. Croak. Croak.*

Grannie motioned for me to sit on the tree stump next to hers. We watched the sun's midmorning rays dance across the water's surface.

Then Grannie picked up a rock and hurled it through the air to the center of the pond. *Plop!* Waves rippled in concentric circles to the pond's edge. First one circle, then another, then another. I was amazed to see that such a small object could make such a difference.

Sooner or later our journey through grief will take us to the pond of relating. We may wander through the wilderness for a while until we see the road sign that points the way. Then we'll realize that our longtime companions— solitude and sadness—have been with us long enough. Now is the time to allow the sunlight to dance across our souls and for us to be with others.

After being with solitude and sadness for so long, we may doubt that our loss can make a difference to anyone else. Then we see a person who is grieving, and we feel at ease sharing about our journey through grief and what we've learned. The person is encouraged and in time may reach out to someone else who is hurting. The cycle continues. One person, then another, then another. As we hurl the rock of our loss into the center of the pond of relating, we see the ripple effects that relating our loss to others can have.

If you're not convinced that you and your loss can have an eternal effect in others' lives, consider Jesus. He invested Himself in twelve men's lives . . . who invested in others . . . who invested in others . . . who invested in others. The ripple effect of His life changed the world, which continues today, even though He is gone physically.

How have others made a ripple effect in your life? How has God already used the loss of your loved one to impact others' lives? How can you allow Him to use you to pass on what you know?

Go ahead. Journey to the pond of relating. Throw in your stone of loss, and watch the ripple effect!

God, show me if this is the time You want me to help others. Thank You for the people who have made a difference in my life. I don't want my loss to be stagnant. Instead, reveal to me how my loved one's life already has touched others'. Show me how I can encourage fellow grievers. Be the Rock in my loss. Help me have an eternal ripple effect on others. Amen.

My Journey

_____

_____

_____

_____

_____

_____

_____

_____

_____

_____

_____

_____

_____

_____

_____

_____

_____

_____

_____

_____

_____

_____

_____

Part 12: Living

YOUR JOURNEY TO LIVING

Living: *to show life, conduct, or manner of life; active; functioning; the power to grow*

My life was suddenly divided into before and after, and there was no going back to before. But then I realized I had a choice to live the after. I had to decide.
—BRENDA NEAL, *A Time to Mourn, a Time to Dance*

"I am way and the truth and the life."
—*John 14:6*

Devotion 49

JOURNEY TO THE
LIGHTHOUSE OF LIVING

"I am the light of the world. Whoever follows me will never walk in darkness, but will have the light of life."

—JOHN 8:12

Ocean waves crash against the shore as fog and darkness move in. Hidden beneath the water's surface lies a minefield of rocks waiting for the unsuspecting ship that sails too close. Then, just as the seafarers near the rocks, a beacon of light pierces through the foggy night as if to say, "Danger! Danger!" The sailors respond to the warning and steer away. The lighthouse has fulfilled its purpose.

Lighthouses have been around since the eighth century BC and usually are constructed at strategic or isolated points on a coastline. They project light at night and by day serve as a marker to safely guide ships sailing in coastal waters. Lighthouses illuminate the darkness, guide away from danger and destruction, and serve as beacons of hope.

At times in our grief journey, we may experience the darkness and get caught in the fog of loss; we may be nearing destruction. Other times we may realize that loss has enlarged our lives, and we can be beacons of hope to others.

Like a lighthouse, we may stand alone in the darkness and fog. Hidden rocks of discouragement, hopelessness, and bitterness lie in wait for unsuspecting people. Lives will be lost unless someone lights the way. "Shine through us to warn others and to guide them safely through," we cry out to God. In this way, we become lighthouses to everyone we meet, proclaiming God's hope and life.

When Jesus said, "I am the light of the world. Whoever follows me will never walk in darkness, but will have the light of life" (John 8:12), He was claiming to be the Light by which truth and falsehood are distinguished. Light reveals reality and destroys the deception and illusion that darkness brings. Jesus' light brings God's presence, protection, and guidance into our lives. He becomes our Lighthouse, illuminating our way.

Look around. A world full of people needs to be guided from death to life. These people need God's presence, protection, and guidance. Your journey through grief has led you this far so you can be a beacon of hope and a lighthouse for the living. Will you be Christ's light today to people in need? Will you allow God to use your experience of loss to radiate hope to others? Embrace living and be a lighthouse, just as God has been for you.

Lord, thank You for being the Light of the World and the Light of life. You are my Lighthouse, who protects and guides me in my journey through grief. You point the way toward living. Illuminate my life with Your truth. Help me be a beacon of hope to others who need encouragement or need to know You. Show me who is in danger of being destroyed and provide opportunities for me to be a lighthouse to guide them to living. Amen.

My Journey

_____

_____

_____

_____

_____

Devotion 50

LIVING WITH NEW
ROLES AND EXPECTATIONS

*Join with me in suffering, like a good soldier of Christ
Jesus. No one serving as a soldier gets entangled in civilian
affairs, but rather tries to please his commanding officer.*

—2 TIMOTHY 2:3–4

While packing for a business trip, Bob surveyed the
piles of clothes, books, and workshop materials
scattered all over the floor and wondered how everything
was going to fit in the suitcase. The last time he had
attempted this feat, he had destroyed his baggage. So reluctantly he decided to leave a few things behind.

Later during his flight, Bob realized that his lug-
gage was similar to his life, bulging with expectations
and about to burst with more responsibilities than any

one person should carry. *But I'm not doing that much,* he rationalized.

He made a list to ease his conscience. To his amazement, he discovered that he was juggling twenty-seven roles. Since his wife's death, Bob had comforted himself by making busyness his constant companion. Maybe it helped to mask his pain, or it distracted him from feeling the void. Whatever the reason, Bob knew he needed to lighten his load, evaluate his expectations, and redefine his roles during this season of his journey.

Bob began by asking himself, *What is my motive for doing what I do—is it my expectations, others' expectations, or God's expectations?* After sifting each of his roles through the grid of this question, he discovered some roles (being a child of God and a dad) only he could fulfill. Many roles, though meaningful and good, could be delegated or deleted during the healing season of his grief journey.

Bob realized that he assumed roles and activities he felt he could control. He wondered if this underlying motive was triggered because he couldn't control his loved one's death. Bob's personal expectations were unrealistic, and he needed to relinquish many of his roles.

It occurred to Bob that experiencing life to the fullest is like using a map. If his map was accurate, he could know where he was, where to go, and how he could get there. If it was false, he would be overwhelmed, misguided, and lost.

Since he was afraid to trust himself or others to guide him, he sought a more reliable map—God's Word. He began to follow the route the Bible prescribed. He prayed more, studied the Bible, listened to God without talking, meditated on the Word, and evaluated his motives based on God's expectations.

As Bob sought truth, he was reminded that Jesus juggled the roles of Mentor, Teacher, Healer, Friend, Evangelist, Carpenter, Child of God, and fellow Griever. He wondered if Jesus ever felt overwhelmed. Because Jesus' motives were pure and His decision-making was rooted in God's expectations, Bob knew that Jesus had chosen to live the right roles. Jesus had set boundaries and priorities and was undeterred by others' expectations. He had made time with God and time for rest and restoration. He had mastered living with expectations that pulled Him in many directions and with a variety of ever-changing roles.

What about you? Is your life bulging with roles and expectations? Is busyness a distraction from your grief? Are you motivated by your expectations, others' expectations, or God's expectations? Maybe you need to evaluate your roles, relinquish unrealistic expectations, and map out a strategy rooted in truth so that you can please God and live the way He intended. Trust me—lightening your load and living with God's expectations is a map worth following.

> God, sometimes I become overwhelmed with all the roles and expectations I juggle. Then I become scared to slow down and let go because I'll feel the pain and void in my life from my loss. A role I once filled is no longer a part of who I am, and that makes me feel lost. Help me evaluate my motives, relinquish inappropriate or unnecessary roles, and map out a strategy based on Your expectations. Guide me through this part of my journey through grief, and help me adjust to new roles. Amen.

My Journey

_____

_____

_____

_____

_____

_____

_____

Devotion 51

BEING THANKFUL IS IN ORDER

Give thanks in all circumstances; for this
is God's will for you in Christ Jesus.
—1 THESSALONIANS 5:18

I was pleasantly surprised when friends provided us with a much-needed family getaway to a bed-and-breakfast in Flagstaff, Arizona, after the loss of our son. The thought of cool temperatures, pine trees, no phones, and no schedules invigorated me. I hadn't felt that way in a long time; it would be just the restoration my soul needed. I could see myself sweater clad, sipping coffee, book in hand, nestled in a rocking chair on the inn's turn-of-the-century front porch. I envisioned time for laughter, naps, family walks, playing games, and meaningful conversations.

Mere minutes after we had checked into our nostalgic suite, I was jolted by reality. "Kath, where's the television?"

My husband's tone of voice told me he wasn't prepared to hear my response.

"This is a place to relax. There is no television," I announced.

"No television? You know that's how I unwind."

It was going to be a long weekend after all.

Relief engulfed me when a train whistle from the nearby depot sounded and seven-year-old Jake asked, "Mom, can we go see the trains now?"

I was determined to have a great time. But by midnight, we realized that the hourly train whistles were a fixture of the place. By 2:00 a.m., we were singing along to the music blaring next door, as our thumps on the wall apparently were being ignored or were unheard by the celebrating guests. By 3:00 a.m., my knock on the neighbors' door and exhausted pleas worked, and we were finally able to sleep.

The seven o'clock train ended our slumber. Rich strode into the bathroom to take his shower, but moments later he bellowed, "There's no water!"

I sought immediate recourse from the innkeepers. They told me the city had failed to notify them about work on the water main. They apologized for the inconvenience. When I reentered our room with this news, I took one look at Rich's face (and hair) and knew I shouldn't suggest breakfast in the inn's formal dining room. Instead, I encouraged Rich to wear a hat, and we went out.

The hour-long wait at the restaurant fueled our frustration, and by the time we were seated at a table, I'm embarrassed to admit that the three of us were barely speaking to one another.

"Mom, I need to go to the bathroom," Jake whined.

"It's your turn, Rich!" I snapped.

Alone at the table, I sipped my coffee and surveyed my dashed expectations for this weekend, only to be interrupted by Rich and Jake's premature return.

Rich sighed. "You're not going to be believe this. The bathroom is out of order!"

We erupted in a trio of laughter. During breakfast we made amends to God and to one another. After we released our expectations, we were able to enjoy the rest of our time together. We were determined to be thankful—no matter what!

God taught me a valuable lesson that weekend. Even when my expectations or circumstances are "out of order," a thankful response is "in order." And that applies not only to bed-and-breakfast accommodations, but also to the grieving process. When we expect to be further along in the process than we are, when our progress seems slow, or when we are jolted back to an earlier stage we thought we had surpassed, our expectations may be out of order. But if we can find within ourselves the wherewithal to be thankful for how far we've come, for how faithful God has been to us, and for the progress we know the Lord will enable us to make, then our response will be in order.

What expectations have caused you to feel frustrated with your grief journey? As you've tried to deal with your loss, what circumstances have caught you by surprise, leaving you feeling confused and hurt? Release your expectations and embrace thankfulness; doing so will make the journey so much easier.

God, I admit that often my expectations are out of order, especially when it comes to grief. Forgive me for the times I'm too hard on myself and others. Help me give thanks in all circumstances and embrace life from Your perspective. Thank You for laughter, friends, family, time away, Your Word, and even for the disappointments You have enabled me to endure. Remind me that You are in control of my living and that being thankful in all circumstances is "in order." Amen.

My Journey

_____

_____

_____

_____

_____

_____

_____

_____

_____

_____

_____

_____

_____

_____

_____

_____

_____

_____

_____

_____

_____

_____

_____

_____

LIVING IN THE FATHER'S ARMS

The eternal God is your refuge, and
underneath are the everlasting arms.
—DEUTERONOMY 33:27

When I was a child, my dad used to take me with him in his gas truck as he made deliveries to farmers in the country. I barely could see over the dashboard, so Dad sat me on a gallon oilcan. When we arrived at our delivery destination, I loved to help him pump the gas into the immense tanks. My ritual was to perch atop the back of the gas truck and watch Dad climb up and down the ladder. I felt safe and secure until the tank was full and I needed to get down. Because I was afraid of heights, fear overshadowed me. It felt too risky to jump.

My dad must have sensed my fear because he always came to my rescue. With a confident smile and outstretched arms, he would coax me to jump. Trembling with fear, I stood at the edge and looked into my dad's eyes. "Jump! I'll catch you," he would repeat.

Somehow I knew I could trust him. I took a deep breath, closed my eyes, and jumped. How comforting to feel his arms wrapped tightly around me! I was safe in my daddy's arms.

You and I reach a point in our journey through grief where we want to enjoy life's scenery, but our view is impaired, and we can't see above the dashboard of our loss. That's when we may receive an unexpected word of encouragement or an act of kindness from others who give us a lift. They may even try to coax us back into the circle of involvement. We want to embrace living, but we're afraid to jump. Fear, guilt, and uncertainty hold us back.

God understands. His Word soothes our anxious hearts. His Spirit calms our fears. If we open our eyes to His presence, we may even sense Him standing there, smiling with outstretched arms. *Jump into living*, He says. *I'll catch you*. Will you trust Him? Will you jump?

As you reflect on your journey through grief, remember that He is with you through your iceberg of denial and your volcano of anger. He helps you wander through the wilderness of "Why?" He walks with you in the marketplace of bargaining, weeps with you through the flash flood of tears, and gives you courage in the fire of surrender. When you journey to the table of acceptance, He offers a tissue and a candle. He is your Mountain Mover as you praise your way through pain and your Transformer in your cocoon of being. He rejoices with you as you celebrate your framed memories and connects with you as you journey to the pond of relating. Why would He leave you now as you get ready to jump into the journey of living? He is the way, the truth, and the life. You can trust Him on this part of your journey through grief too. He's waiting to catch you. Go ahead: jump!

Living in the Father's arms is the best place to be now and for all eternity. Are you certain that you will live with Him in heaven, where death, pain, tears, and sorrow no longer exist? Make sure of that today. Choose living.

Everlasting Father, thank You for being with me on my journey through grief. Your light and companionship comfort me. I'm ready to embrace living, but I'm anxious and afraid. Replace my fear with faith and my trembling with trust. Help me jump into Your arms. I need You in my life right now. I believe that You are the way, the truth, and the life and that You stretched out Your arms on the cross and died for me. You overcame death, rose again, and are preparing a place for me to live eternally with You. I look forward to being in heaven with You. Today I commit to live in Your arms forever. Amen.

My Journey

_____

_____

_____

_____

_____

_____

_____

_____

_____

_____

_____

_____

_____

_____

_____

A NOTE FROM THE AUTHOR

*D*ear Reader,

Thank you for taking the time to journey through the pages of this book. When I first began writing it in 1998, I was early in my journey of grieving the loss of my son and two other babies through miscarriage. I was also pregnant and daily fighting fear of losing another child as I wrote. You, the reader, inspired me to keep trusting and stay focused on the outcome of spreading hope and changing lives. I had you taped on the wall above my computer. Hand-sketched stick figures on paper reminded me daily of others who were grieving and of the need for this book. By God's grace and power, and with the support of many who prayed for and encouraged me, I completed the manuscript and delivered a healthy son, Joshua.

Looking back through the years, I'm humbled by the multitudes of readers and support-group leaders around the world whom I've connected with online or in person when I spoke who have shared how God has used this book to comfort them and bring hope. I'm in awe of how God has transformed my hurt into hope to help others and of how the need for this book continues. I'm also surprised at how many times through the years I've read these devotions to seek God's comfort for myself when I lost more loved ones and a close friend.

I'm grateful to those past and present who have supported me in the journey of writing and updating this book: my PIT Team (Personal Intercessory Team); my 2000 Zondervan team and my 2016 HarperCollins team; my contributors who have shared insights about grief or allowed me to share their personal story; my writing mentors John McAdam, Carol Kent, and Judy Couchman; my friends CBWA, Lisa Jernigan, Jan James, and the women from Hopelifters; my husband, Rich, and my sons, Jake, Josh, and Jordan. And to my Lord and Savior, Jesus Christ: may He be glorified and may eternal hope spread.

Amazingly, as I finish the 2016 updates for this book, I've been journeying through a health crisis with my eighty-year-old mother, Alice, who lives several hundred miles away. Her failing health required me to put my updates on hold, fly to the Midwest, and live in the hospital by her side for two weeks. My mom has been a prayer champion for this book, past and present, and even now from her long distance hospital "war room," she is praying for me and for you. Perhaps God's timing for this revision is preparing my heart to journey through grieving for my mom as she prepares for her life in eternity.

I pray that the God of compassion who has comforted you will work in and through you to comfort others and that you will spread hope to others who are hurting or pass along a copy of this book to someone else.

Your hopelifter,
Kathe Wunnenberg
Proverbs 3:5–6

About the Author

*K*athe Wunnenberg is a hopelifter. She believes God can use anything you offer Him and transform it into hope to help others. Known for her visionary leadership, mentoring, creativity, and compassion-in-action lifestyle, Kathe is a communicator and connector who loves to offer biblical solutions and practical resources for real-life problems. God has sustained her through numerous life challenges including infertility, adoption, miscarriages, carrying a child with a fatal birth defect, the loss of a child, birthing babies in her forties, depression, and starting and leading a ministry.

Kathe is the author of *Grieving the Loss of a Loved One*, *Grieving the Child I Never Knew*, *Longing for a Child*, and *Hopelifter: Creative Ways to Spread Hope When Life Hurts*. She is the founder and president of Hopelifters Unlimited and lives in Phoenix, Arizona, with her husband. They have three living sons and four children in heaven. To learn more, connect with Kathe at www.hopelifters.com, or follow her on Facebook at Hopelifters Unlimited or Twitter @hopelifters.

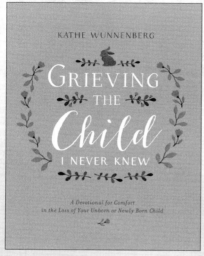

(ISBN 9780310350651)   (ISBN 9780310320159)

In the midst of life's most difficult circumstances, God desires to be your Comforter. *Grieving the Child I Never Knew* and *Hopelifter* will remind you of His constant presence and renew your hope in Him.

Available at bookstores everywhere.